Sams **Teach Yourself**

Google Analytics™

in **10 Minutes**

Trademarks

All terms mentioned in this book that are known to be trademarks or service marks have been appropriately capitalized. Sams Publishing cannot attest to the accuracy of this information. Use of a term in this book should not be regarded as affecting the validity of any trademark or service mark.

Warning and Disclaimer

Every effort has been made to make this book as complete and as accurate as possible, but no warranty or fitness is implied. The information provided is on an "as is" basis. The author and the publisher shall have neither liability nor responsibility to any person or entity with respect to any loss or damages arising from the information contained in this book.

Bulk Sales

Sams Publishing offers excellent discounts on this book when ordered in quantity for bulk purchases or special sales. For more information, please contact

> **U.S. Corporate and Government Sales**
> **1-800-382-3419**
> corpsales@pearsontechgroup.com

For sales outside of the U.S., please contact

> **International Sales**
> international@pearson.com

Associate Publisher
Greg Wiegand

Senior Acquisitions Editor
Katherine Bull

Managing Editor
Kristy Hart

Project Editor
Anne Goebel

Copy Editor
WaterCrest Publishing

Indexer
Sheila Schroeder

Proofreader
Karen A. Gill

Technical Editor
Jenna DeMarco

Publishing Coordinator
Cindy Teeters

Cover Designer
Gary Adair

Compositor
Jake McFarland

Contents at a Glance

Table of Contents

Dedication

To Sherry: Ten minutes is never enough.

About the Author

Michael Miller has written more than 100 nonfiction books over the past two decades. His best-selling titles include *Sams Teach Yourself YouTube in 10 Minutes*, *Sams Teach Yourself Wikipedia in 10 Minutes*, *Windows 7 Your Way*, *Googlepedia: The Ultimate Google Resource*, *Using Google AdWords and AdSense*, *The Complete Idiot's Guide to Search Engine Optimization*, and *The Ultimate Web Marketing Guide*. He has established a reputation for practical advice, technical accuracy, and an unerring empathy for the needs of his readers. For more information about Mr. Miller and his writing, visit his website at www.molehillgroup.com or email him at ga@molehillgroup.com.

Acknowledgments

Special thanks to the usual suspects at Sams, including but not limited to Greg Wiegand, Katherine Bull, Sarah Kearns, and Anne Goebel. Thanks as well to technical editors Jim Snyder and Peter Howley of Empirical Path Consulting, who helped ensure the technical accuracy of this book.

We Want to Hear from You!

As the reader of this book, *you* are our most important critic and commentator. We value your opinion and want to know what we're doing right, what we could do better, what areas you'd like to see us publish in, and any other words of wisdom you're willing to pass our way.

You can email or write me directly to let me know what you did or didn't like about this book—as well as what we can do to make our books stronger.

Please note that I cannot help you with technical problems related to the topic of this book, and that due to the high volume of mail I receive, I might not be able to reply to every message.

When you write, please be sure to include this book's title and author as well as your name and phone or email address. I will carefully review your comments and share them with the author and editors who worked on the book.

E-mail: consumer@samspublishing.com

Mail: Greg Wiegand
Associate Publisher
Sams Publishing
800 East 96th Street
Indianapolis, IN 46240 USA

Reader Services

Visit our website and register this book at www.informit.com/title/
9780672333200 for convenient access to any updates, downloads, or
errata that might be available for this book.

Introduction

Is your website performing as well as it should? Are you retaining visitors—or losing them too fast? Are you converting lookers to buyers—or are they bouncing from your site before they finish the checkout process?

When you want to find out more about the people visiting your website, turn to Google Analytics. Google Analytics is a free tool offered by Google that generates detailed statistics about website visitors. This tool—actually, a series of detailed reports—tracks visitors from all referring sources, including search engines, pay-per-click (PPC) advertising networks (such as Google AdWords), display advertisements, email marketing, and other channels. It tells you how visitors found your site—and if they came from a search engine, just what they were searching for.

But that's not all. Google Analytics tells you what pages these people visit on your site, how long they view each page, and where they exit your site. It's information that is both interesting and useful; Google Analytics is a great tool for improving the effectiveness of any website.

The problem is that Google Analytics offers so much detailed data, it's hard to keep it all straight. There's so much there, it's overwhelming. How do you know what report holds the information you need? And how do you customize Google Analytics to work best with your specific pages?

That's where this book comes in. *Sams Teach Yourself Google Analytics in 10 Minutes* is a quick-and-easy way to learn how to use Google Analytics to analyze and improve your website. Every lesson in this book is short and to the point, so you can learn everything you need to learn at your own pace, in your own time. Just follow the straightforward *Sams Teach Yourself in 10 Minutes* game plan: short, goal-oriented lessons that can make you productive with each topic in 10 minutes or less.

What You Need to Know Before You Use This Book

How much prior experience do you need before starting this book? Well, it helps if you have some sort of experience in web marketing, so terms like click-through rate and pageviews aren't totally foreign. And a little familiarity with HTML might be useful, as Google Analytics requires you to insert (and, in some instances, modify) brief snippets of code into your web pages to activate its tracking functionality. Of course, you can always have someone else on your team do the HTML work; you don't have to be a coding wizard to do what you need to do. Beyond these basic skills, no prior experience with Google Analytics (or with any web analytics service) is presumed.

About the *Sams Teach Yourself in 10 Minutes* Series

Sams Teach Yourself Google Analytics in 10 Minutes uses a series of short lessons that walk you through the various features of Google Analytics. Each lesson is designed to take about 10 minutes, and each is limited to a particular operation or group of features. Most of the instruction is presented in easy-to-follow numbered steps, and there are plenty of examples and screen shots to show you what things look like along the way. By the time you finish this book, you should feel confident in using Google Analytics to analyze—and improve—your website.

Special Sidebars

In addition to the normal text and figures, you find what we call *sidebars* scattered throughout that highlight special kinds of information. These are intended to help you save time and to teach you important information fast.

CAUTION: Cautions alert you to common mistakes and tell you how to avoid them.

TIP: Tips explain inside hints for using Google Analytics more efficiently.

NOTE: Notes present pertinent pieces of information related to the surrounding discussion.

LESSON 1

A 10-Minute Guide to Web Analytics

In this lesson, you learn what web analytics is—and what it does.

Understanding Web Analytics

When you want to know more about who is visiting your website and what they're doing there, you need web analytics. But what is this thing called web analytics?

Put simply, *web analytics* is the collection and analysis of data relating to website visitors. It's a way to measure the traffic to your website and then find out what visitors are doing during their visits.

What kind of data are measured? Web analytics tracks such metrics as pageviews, visits, unique visitors, and the like. The resulting analysis examines both the quantity and quality of visitors to a site.

The goal of web analytics is to better understand how a website is being used—and apply that information to optimize the site's usage. It's more than just basic data collection; it's an attempt to learn more about how people use a site, and why.

Why Analyze Website Traffic?

If you run a website, why might you want to employ web analytics?

It's simple: Web analytics helps you better understand the visitors to your site. Analytics tracks visitor behavior, so that you have a better idea what your site's visitors are doing—and why. With the right analytics package, you can discover the following:

▶ How many visitors your site attracts.

▶ Where your visitors came from—which sites directed the most traffic to your site, as well as where geographically your visitors are located.

▶ How long visitors are staying on your site.

▶ What pages visitors visit first—and which they visit last before they leave.

▶ If visitors came to your site from a search engine, what keywords they searched that brought up your site in their search results.

▶ If visitors came to your site from an advertisement, where that ad was placed—and what percentage of visitors who clicked on your ad viewed key pages or completed transactions.

▶ What types of web browsers your visitors are using—so you can better design your site to look good with those browsers.

Who Uses Web Analytics?

You might think that web analytics, like other forms of market research, is used primarily by big companies. That isn't true, however. Web analytics is for any size company or website; a small personal website has access to the same statistics as does a large corporate one.

In fact, any website can benefit from knowing more about its visitors. Websites both large and small can use web analytics to determine where new visitors are coming from and tailor the site's content to those sources. It's valuable data, no matter the size of your site—or the amount of traffic it attracts.

And, while web analytics is a great tool for marketing research, it isn't limited to use by a company's marketing department. A company's IT department, for example, can use analytic data to forecast server load and budget appropriately for new equipment purchases; a sales department can use analytic data to determine the effectiveness of various promotions and placements.

> **NOTE: More Than Just Websites**
>
> You can use web analytics to track not just traditional websites, but also blogs, podcasts, online videos, web-based advertisements, and the like.

How Web Analytics Works

When it comes to tracking web visitors, there are two fundamental types of analytics:

- ▶ **Onsite analytics** uses site-specific data to track visitors to a specific website.

- ▶ **Offsite analytics** uses Internet-wide information to determine the most visited sites on the web.

Offsite analytics is used to compile industry-wide analysis, while onsite analytics is used to report on individual website performance. Website owners and webmasters are most interested in onsite analytics; this is the type of analytics we discuss primarily in this book.

Onsite analytics works by utilizing a technique known as *page tagging*. This technique places a "bug," in the form of a bit of JavaScript code, in the basic HTML code for a web page. This embedded code collects certain information about the page and its visitors. This information is then passed on to a web analytics service, which collates the data and uses it to create various analytic reports.

Beyond Data Collection: Using Web Analytics Data

It may be interesting to know how many people visit your site each month, as well as what sites drove the most traffic to yours, but how can you put this data to good use?

The key is to analyze the data about what happened in the past to both predict and influence what happens in the future. That is, you can use web analytics data to make informed decisions about your website strategy.

Examine the data to determine what is and isn't working on your site; then use that information to play up your site's strengths and improve its weaknesses. If you know, for example, that a particular page is pulling a lot of traffic from Google and other search engines, you expand on that page's content to attract even more of that traffic. Or if you determine that visitors are leaving too soon after viewing a given page—that is, if there's nothing there to keep them sticking around—you can work to improve that page's content to be more valuable to visitors.

> TIP: **Trends Matter**
> When examining web analytics data, it's tempting to get engrossed by all the raw data available. Although individual numbers are important, it's more important to examine longer-term trends. For example, it's more important to examine how the number of visitors is changing over time than it is to obsess over a single visitor number.

Web Analytics and Internet Advertising

Web analytics is also valuable if you're purchasing advertising on the Internet, especially pay-per-click (PPC) advertising. You can track and analyze which campaigns result in the most conversions from clicks to actual sales. And if you're advertising on Google's AdWords, you can track which keywords are triggering the most ad displays and which ads have the highest click-through rate.

In other words, you can use web analytics to track the effectiveness of each ad you place. With proper analysis, you can learn which ads are driving the most potential customers and which ads aren't pulling their weight. That information will help you better place ads in your next campaign; you fine-tune your advertising strategy over time.

Without web analytics, you have no idea which ads are working and which aren't. You learn from both your successes and your failures.

Understanding Key Metrics

There are many different data points that can be collected via web analytics. Some of these data points, or metrics, might be familiar to you; others may not. To that end, Table 1.1 details some of the most important of these metrics and what they measure.

TABLE 1.1   Key Web Analytics Metrics

Metric	Description
% exit	The percentage of users who exit from a given web page as a share of pageviews.
Bounce rate	The percentage of visits in which the visitor enters and exits on the same page, without visiting any other pages on the site in between.
Click	A single instance of a visitor clicking a link from one page to another on the same site.
Click path	The sequence of clicks that website visitors follow on a given site.
Click-through rate (CTR)	The percentage of people who view an item and then click it; calculated by dividing the number of clicks by the number of impressions.
Depth of visit (pageviews per session)	The average number of pageviews a visitor initiates before ending his session; calculated by dividing the total number of pageviews by the total number of sessions.
First visit	The first visit from a visitor who has not previously visited the site.

TABLE 1.1   Key Web Analytics Metrics

Metric	Description
Hit	A request for a file from a web server. Note that a hit is *not* the same as a pageview; a single page can have multiple elements (images, text boxes, and so forth) that need to be individually loaded from the server. For example, a web page that includes four images would result in five hits to the server.
Impression	A single display of an advertisement on a web page.
Loyalty	A measurement of how often visitors come to a website, calculated by dividing the total number of sessions or visits by the total number of unique visitors.
New visitor	A visitor who has not made previous visits to a website.
Pageview	A display of a complete web page. One visitor looking at a single page on your site generates one pageview. (Pageviews typically don't include error pages, or those pages viewed by web crawlers or robots.)
Pageview duration (time on page)	The average amount of time that visitors spend on each page of a website.
Repeat visitor	A visitor who has made at least one previous visit to a website.
Session	A series of pageviews from the same visitor with no more than 30 minutes between pageviews—and with no visits to other sites between pageviews. Unlike a visit, a session ends when a visitor opens a page on another site.
Single page visit	A visit from a visitor where only a single page is viewed.
Time on site or length of visit	The average amount of time that visitors spend on a website each time they visit.

TABLE 1.1   Key Web Analytics Metrics

Metric	Description
Unique visitor	A visitor who visits your site one or more times within a given timeframe, typically a single 24-hour period; a visitor can make multiple visits during that timeframe, but this counts as just a single unique visitor. For example, a user visiting your site twice in one day is counted as a single unique visitor.
Visit	A series of pageviews from the same visitor with no more than 30 minutes between each pageview. Unlike a session, a visit continues (for 30 minutes) even after a visitor leaves your site.

NOTE: **PPC Metrics**

When tracking PPC ad performance, additional metrics come into play. These include cost-per-click (CPC), average position, conversions, conversion rate, and the like. (Learn more in Lesson 12, "Tracking Ecommerce.")

Getting to Know Google Analytics

There are many firms that offer web analytics tools and services. One of the most popular is Google Analytics, part of the vast Google empire. Google Analytics is unusually comprehensive in the metrics it tracks; it's also relatively easy to use and completely free.

Because of its cost (or lack of), Google Analytics is popular with websites both large and small. Google Analytics is powerful enough to track traffic at large websites, but easy enough for smaller sites to implement. It tracks all the key metrics detailed in Table 1.1 and more, displaying its results in a series of "Dashboards" and custom reports, like the one shown in Figure 1.1.

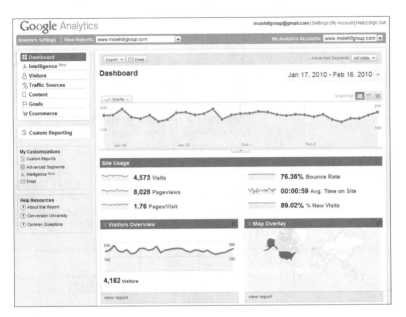

FIGURE 1.1   The main Google Analytics Dashboard.

Google Analytics utilizes onsite analytics to track visitor behavior on a specific site. After you register your site with Google Analytics, Google generates a unique piece of JavaScript code for your site. You then copy and paste this code into the underlying HTML of each site on your page you want to track; once embedded, this code tracks visitor behavior and transmits that data back to Google, where it is analyzed and displayed.

As noted, Google Analytics is completely free. There is no charge to track the performance of your website, nor to access the reports generated by Google Analytics.

Summary

In this lesson, you learned how web analytics works and why you should use this key metric to track visitor behavior on your website. In the next lesson, you learn how to sign up for the Google Analytics program.

LESSON 2

Creating a Google Analytics Account

In this lesson, you learn how to sign up for Google Analytics.

Creating a Google Account

Before you can sign up for Google Analytics, you must have a Google account. If you use Gmail, Google Calendar, Google Docs, or similar Google applications, you already have a Google account and can use that account to sign up for Google Analytics. Likewise, if you subscribe to Google's AdSense or AdWords programs, you can use that account to sign up for Google Analytics.

> NOTE: **Google Account**
> Singing up for a Google account is free. You can then use the same username (your email address) and password to access all of Google's services.

If you do not use any of Google's services, however, you need to create a new Google account. Follow these steps:

1. Go to the Google Analytics main page (www.google.com/analytics/), shown in Figure 2.1, and click the Sign Up Now link.

2. When the Create an Account page appears, as shown in Figure 2.2, enter your email address into the Your Current Email Address box.

3. Create a password and enter it into the Choose a Password box; then enter it again into the Re-Enter Password box.

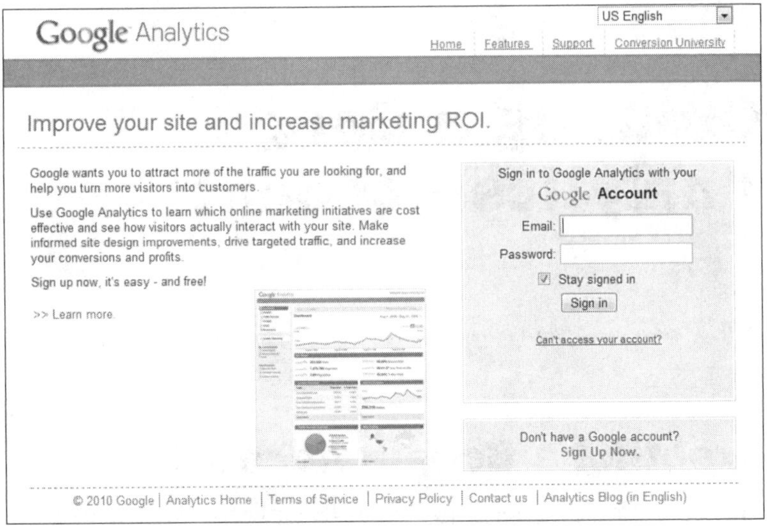

FIGURE 2.1   The Google Analytics main page—before you sign up or sign in.

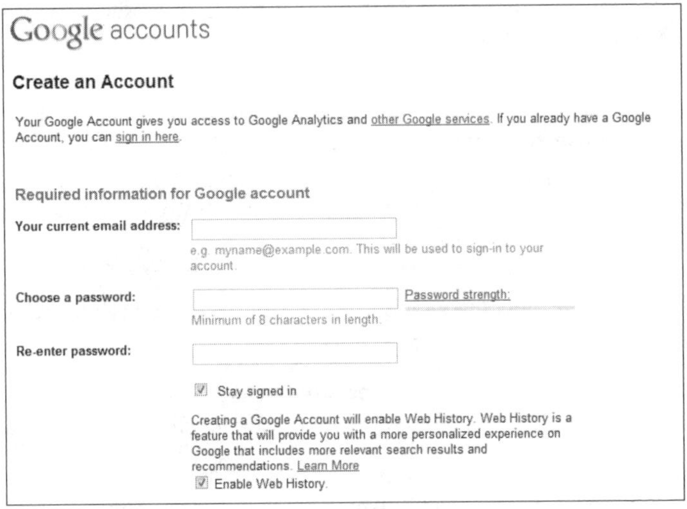

FIGURE 2.2   Creating a new Google account.

4. Select your location from the Location pull-down list.

5. Enter your birthday into the Birthday box.

6. Enter the "secret word" into the Word Verification box.

7. Click the I Accept. Create My Account button.

You are now prompted to create your Google Analytics account, which we discuss in the following section.

Signing Up for Google Analytics

Once you've created a Google account, you can then sign up for the Google Analytics program. We'll show how to do this from the main Google Analytics page. Follow these steps:

> **NOTE: Continuous Signup**
>
> If you're signing up for Google Analytics at the same time you're creating a Google account, go directly to Step 4 after creating your Google account.

1. Go to the Google Analytics main page (www.google.com/analytics/) and click the Sign Up Now link.

2. When the next page appears, enter your Google account email address and password; then click the Sign In button.

3. When the Getting Started page appears, click the Sign Up button.

4. You now see the General Information page, shown in Figure 2.3. Enter the URL for your site's home page into the Website's URL box.

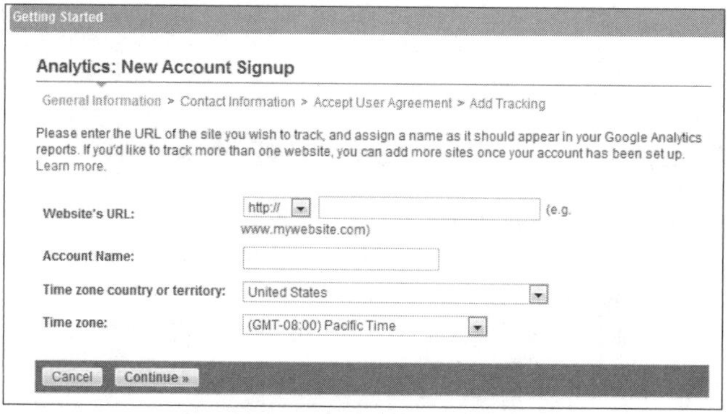

FIGURE 2.3   Entering information about your website.

> NOTE: **Secure Sites**
>
> If your site is a secure site, pull down the list and select **https://**
> instead of the default **http://**.

5. Enter a name for this website into the Account Name box.

> NOTE: **Account Name**
>
> You should select an account name that helps you identify this site
> if you plan on tracking multiple sites with Google Analytics—the
> domain name or home page URL, the internal name you give to the
> site, or something similar.

6. Select your country from the Time Zone Country or Territory
pull-down list.

7. Select your time zone from the Time Zone pull-down list.

8. Click the Continue button.

9. When the Contact Information page appears, as shown in Figure
2.4, enter your first name and last name into the appropriate
boxes.

Getting Started

Analytics: New Account Signup

General Information > Contact Information > Accept User Agreement > Add Tracking

Last Name:

First Name:

Country or territory: Please select your country or territory

« Back   Continue »

FIGURE 2.4   Entering your contact information.

10. Select your country (again) from the Country or Territory pull-
down list.

11. Click the Continue button.

12. When the Accept User Agreement page appears, read the terms of service and check the Yes option.

13. Click the Create New Account button.

14. Google now displays the tracking code you need to add to your website, as shown in Figure 2.5. You should copy and paste this code as detailed in Lesson 3, "Adding Google Analytics to Your Website."

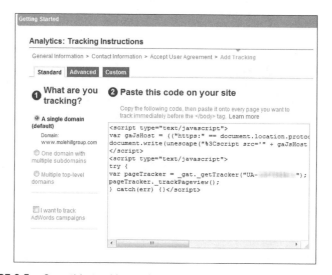

FIGURE 2.5   Copy this tracking code to your website's HTML.

15. After you've copied the tracking code, click the Save and Finish button.

Summary

In this lesson, you learned how to sign up for Google Analytics. In the next lesson, you learn how to add the Google Analytics tracking code to your website.

LESSON 3

Adding Google Analytics to Your Website

In this lesson, you learn how to configure your website for monitoring with Google Analytics.

Adding Your Website to Google Analytics

As you learned in Lesson 2, "Creating a Google Analytics Account," Google asks you questions about your website during the initial signup process and then generates a piece of tracking code for you to paste into your website's underlying HTML. We'll review that process here, starting with your clicking the Sign Up button.

1. From the General Information page, shown in Figure 3.1, enter the URL for your site's home page into the Website's URL box.

2. Enter a name for this website into the Account Name box.

3. Select your country from the Time Zone Country or Territory pull-down list.

4. Select your time zone from the Time Zone pull-down list.

5. Click the Continue button.

6. When the Contact Information page appears, enter your first name and last name into the appropriate boxes.

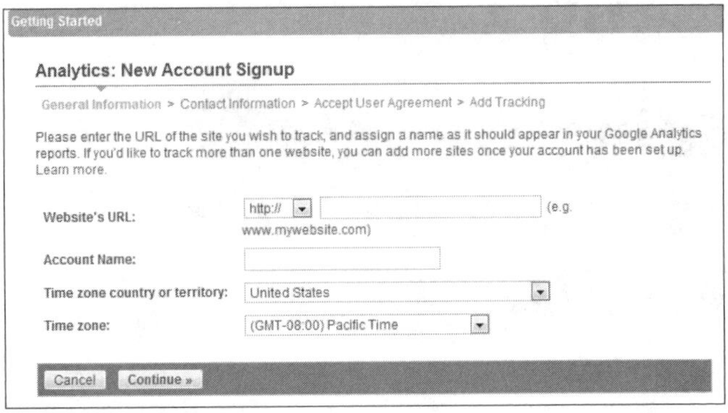

FIGURE 3.1 Entering information about your website.

7. Select your country (again) from the Country or Territory pull-down list.

8. Click the Continue button.

9. When the Accept User Agreement page appears, read the terms of service and check the Yes option.

10. By default, Google shares your site's analytics data with AdWords, AdSense, and other Google products, as well as anonymously with Google and other sites for benchmarking services. If you do not want to share your data, click the Edit Settings link in the Data Sharing Settings section; then uncheck the two sharing options.

11. Click the Create New Account button.

12. When the next page appears, as shown in Figure 3.2, select what you want to track: a single domain (that is, a single website), one domain with multiple subdomains, or multiple top-level domains.

13. If you also want to track AdWords advertising campaigns, check the I Want to Track AdWords Campaigns option.

14. Google now displays the tracking code you need to add to your website. Highlight and copy this tracking code.

15. Click the Save and Finish button.

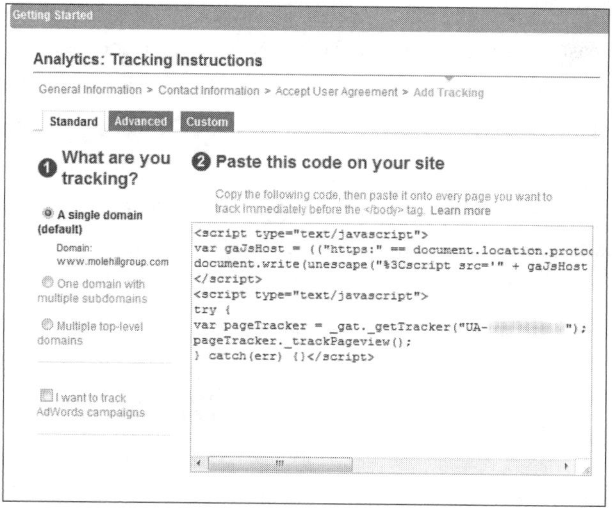

FIGURE 3.2   Copy this tracking code to your website's HTML.

Adding Google Analytics Code to Your Website

The tracking code generated by Google Analytics is a piece of JavaScript that looks something like this:

```
<script type="text/javascript">
var gaJsHost = (("https:" == document.location.protocol) ?
"https://ssl." : "http://www.");
document.write(unescape("%3Cscript src='" + gaJsHost + "google-
analytics.com/ga.js' type='text/javascript'%3E%3C/script%3E"));
</script>

<script type="text/javascript">
try{
var pageTracker = _gat._getTracker("UA-xxxxxx-x");
pageTracker._trackPageview();
} catch(err) {}
</script>
```

As you can see, this code is actually two separate scripts. For your specific code, the "xxxxxx-x" is replaced with your own Google Analytics account number.

Once you've copied the tracking code generated by Google Analytics, you need to paste that code into your website's underlying source code. You need to paste this code into every page on your site that you want to track.

The tracking code should be inserted at the end of your page's **<BODY>** section, just before the **</BODY>** closing tag. Follow these steps:

1. Open the web page in a website editing tool, and enable HTML editing, as opposed to "what you see is what you get" (WYSIWIG) editing.

2. Scroll to the bottom of the document, to the end of the **<BODY>** section.

3. Paste the Google Analytics copy code just before the **</BODY>** tag.

4. Save your web page.

> NOTE: **Dynamic Websites**
> For database-driven dynamic websites, you should insert the tracking code on your **index.php** or equivalent page.

Tracking Blog Performance

You can also use Google Analytics to track performance of a blog. Simply treat your blog as a normal web page when creating a new Google Analytics profile; enter the blog's URL when asked for the website URL.

When Google Analytics generates the tracking code, enter that code into the underlying HTML for the bottom of the blog's main page. This process differs from blog host to blog host. If your blog is hosted by Blogger, here's how it works:

1. After you've generated and copied the Google Analytics tracking code, open your Blogger Dashboard (www.blogger.com), shown in Figure 3.3, and click the Layout link for the blog you want to track.

2. When the Layout page appears, scroll down to the bottom of the page and click the Add a Gadget link beneath the blog postings, as shown in Figure 3.4.

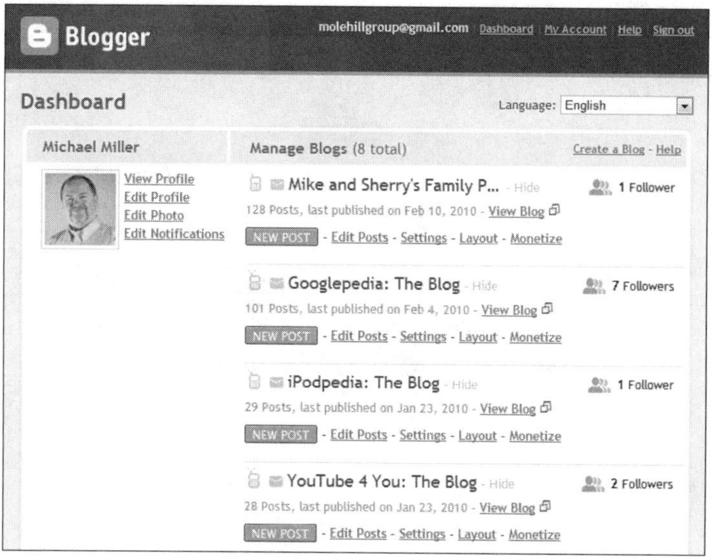

FIGURE 3.3 Editing a blog from the Blogger Dashboard.

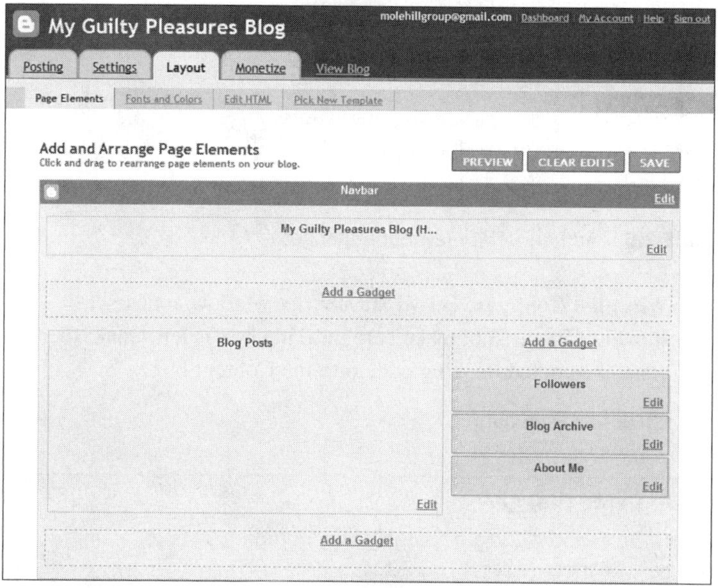

FIGURE 3.4 Add a new gadget to the bottom of your blog.

CAUTION: **No Sidebar Gadgets**

Do not add the tracking code to a sidebar gadget. It must be added to a gadget in the footer of the blog.

3. When the Add a Gadget window appears, as shown in Figure 3.5, click the + for the HTML/JavaScript item.

FIGURE 3.5   Add an HTML/JavaScript gadget.

4. When the Configure HTML/JavaScript window appears, as shown in Figure 3.6, make sure the Title box is left blank; then paste the copied tracking code into the Content box.

5. Click the Save button.

NOTE: **Using Blogger**

Learn more about Blogger blogs in my companion book, *Using Blogger* (Michael Miller, Que, 2010).

FIGURE 3.6   Paste the Google Analytics tracking code into this window.

Regenerating the Tracking Code

What if you don't copy the tracking code when it's first generated? Fortunately, Google allows you to regenerate the tracking code at any time, when it's more convenient for you to paste into your website.

To regenerate the tracking code, follow these steps:

1. Log onto Google Analytics to view the Overview page, shown in Figure 3.7.

2. Identify the website you want, and click that site's Edit link in the Actions column.

3. When the Profile Settings page appears, as shown in Figure 3.8, click the Check Status link at the top right of the page.

4. Google now displays the tracking code for this site. Copy and paste this code into your site's home page, as previously discussed.

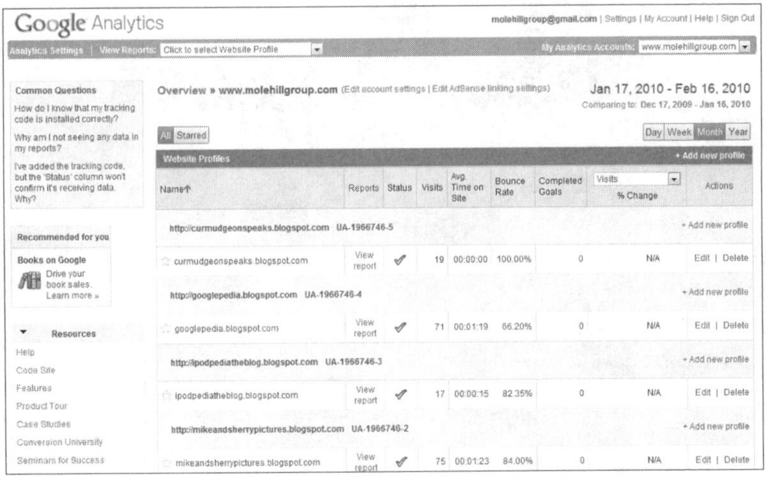

FIGURE 3.7 The Google Analytics Overview page; click the Edit link for the site you want.

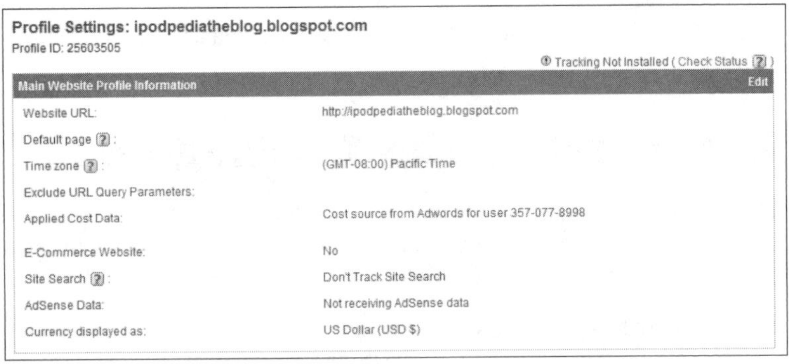

FIGURE 3.8 Click the Check Status link to regenerate the site's tracking code.

Adding Another Website to Google Analytics

You can track more than one website in your Google Analytics account—up to 50 sites, in fact. Each site you track is listed on your Overview page.

To add another website to your account, follow these steps:

1. From the Google Analytics Overview page, click the Add New Profile link.

2. When the Create New Website Profile page appears, as shown in Figure 3.9, check the Add a Profile for a New Domain link.

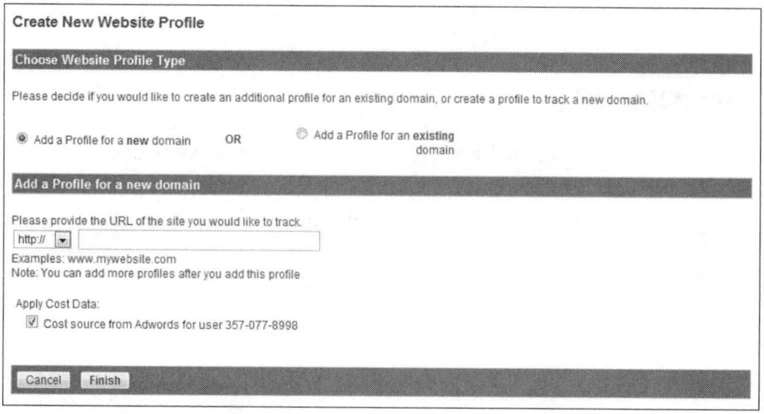

Create New Website Profile

Choose Website Profile Type

Please decide if you would like to create an additional profile for an existing domain, or create a profile to track a new domain.

○ Add a Profile for a **new** domain   OR   ○ Add a Profile for an **existing** domain

Add a Profile for a new domain

Please provide the URL of the site you would like to track.
| http:// ▼ | |
Examples: www.mywebsite.com
Note: You can add more profiles after you add this profile

Apply Cost Data:
☑ Cost source from Adwords for user 357-077-8998

[Cancel] [Finish]

FIGURE 3.9   Adding a new website to your Google Analytics profile.

3. Enter the URL for your site into the appropriate box.

NOTE: **Secure Sites**
If your site is a secure site, pull down the list and select **https://** instead of the default **http://**.

4. Select your country from the Time Zone Country or Territory pull-down list.

5. Select your time zone from the Time Zone pull-down list.

6. Click the Continue button.

7. When the next page appears, select what you want to track: a single domain, one domain with multiple subdomains, or multiple top-level domains.

8. If you also want to track AdWords advertising campaigns, check the I Want to Track AdWords Campaigns option.

9. Google now displays the tracking code you need to add to your website. Copy and paste this code into your site's home page, as discussed previously in this lesson.

10. Click the Save and Finish button.

Summary

In this lesson, you learned how to add the Google Analytics tracking code to your website. In the next lesson, you learn how to use the Google Analytics Dashboard to learn more about your site's performance.

LESSON 4

Using the Google Analytics Dashboard

In this lesson, you learn how to navigate the Google Analytics Overview page and Dashboard.

Navigating from the Overview Page

When you go to www.google.com/analytics/ and enter your email address and password to sign into the site, you see the Overview page, shown in Figure 4.1. This page lists all the sites (profiles you've

Overview » www.molehillgroup.com (Edit account settings | Edit AdSense linking settings)							Jan 17, 2010 - Feb 16, 2010	
							Comparing to: Dec 17, 2009 - Jan 16, 2010	
All Starred							Day Week Month Year	
Website Profiles							+ Add new profile	
Name	Reports	Status	Visits	Avg. Time on Site	Bounce Rate	Completed Goals ↓	Visits ▾ % Change	Actions
http://www.molehillgroup.com UA-1966746-1								+ Add new profile
☆ www.molehillgroup.com	View report	✔	4,573	00:00:59	76.36%	108	⬆ 2.83%	Edit | Delete
http://curmudgeonspeaks.blogspot.com UA-1966746-5								+ Add new profile
☆ curmudgeonspeaks.blogspot.com	View report	✔	19	00:00:00	100.00%	0	N/A	Edit | Delete
http://googlepedia.blogspot.com UA-1966746-4								+ Add new profile
☆ googlepedia.blogspot.com	View report	✔	71	00:01:19	66.20%	0	N/A	Edit | Delete
http://ipodpediatheblog.blogspot.com UA-1966746-3								+ Add new profile
☆ ipodpediatheblog.blogspot.com	View report	✔	17	00:00:15	82.35%	0	N/A	Edit | Delete

FIGURE 4.1   The Google Analytics Overview page.

registered with Google Analytics, along with basic information about each site's performance).

NOTE: **Multiple Accounts**

If your email address accesses more than one account, when you sign into Google Analytics, you see a page that lists each of your accounts. Click an account name to see the Overview page for that account.

For each site, Google Analytics displays the following columns of information:

▶ **Name.** The name or web address of the site.

▶ **Reports.** Click the View Report link to access this site's Dashboard, as discussed later in this lesson.

▶ **Status.** A green checkmark indicates that the tracking code is correctly installed and that Google Analytics is receiving data from this site. A yellow caution triangle indicates that Google Analytics is *not* receiving data from this site; the tracking code may not be properly installed.

▶ **Visits.** The number of visits to this site recorded during the selected timeframe.

▶ **Avg Time on Site.** The amount of time, in minutes and seconds, of an average visit on this site.

▶ **Bounce Rate.** The percentage of visits in which a visitor leaves the site without visiting a second page. (A lower bounce rate is better.)

▶ **Completed Goals.** The number of completions of those goals you've set up for a site. (We'll learn more about goals in Lesson 14, "Setting Up Goals and Funnels.")

▶ **% Change.** The percentage change, up or down, in the selected metric during the selected timeframe. You can display % Change for Visits, Avg. Time on Site, Bounce Rate, or Completed Goals; simply pull down the list and select the metric.

► **Actions.** This column lets you either edit or delete a site profile from your Google Analytics account.

You can change the timeframe for which these data are displayed by clicking the Day, Week, Month, or Year buttons on the top-right side of the page.

NOTE: **Finding Profiles**

By default, the Overview page displays all profiles you've associated with your account. If you have a large number of profiles registered, you can search for specific ones by using the Find Profile box.

Discovering the Dashboard

Detailed information for each of your websites is displayed on a separate Dashboard page. You access the Dashboard for a given website by following these steps:

1. Sign into your Google Analytics account and access the Overview page.

2. Click the View Report link in the Reports column for the selected website.

As you can see in Figure 4.2, the Dashboard is an overview of your site's performance. It includes several graphs and tables that present key metrics in an easily grasped manner. It's also your link to more detailed reporting, which we'll discuss throughout this book.

What do you find in the Dashboard? From roughly top to bottom, we'll detail the major sections of the page.

Overview Graph

By default, the overview graph at the top of the Dashboard page, shown in Figure 4.3, charts the number of visits to your site over the past month.

FIGURE 4.2   The Google Analytics Dashboard.

FIGURE 4.3   The Dashboard overview graph.

You can display other data (pageviews, pages/visit, average time on site, bounce rate, and percent of new visits) by clicking the button on the top left of the graph.

> TIP: **Data Points**
>
> You can display the tracked data for a specific date by hovering your cursor over the data point for that day on the graph.

Site Usage Table

Directly beneath the overview graph is the Site Usage table, shown in Figure 4.4. This table displays a number of key metrics that track your site's performance, including the following:

Site Usage		
4,573 Visits		**76.36%** Bounce Rate
8,028 Pageviews		**00:00:59** Avg. Time on Site
1.76 Pages/Visit		**89.02%** % New Visits

FIGURE 4.4   The Site Usage table.

- ▶ **Visits.** The total number of unique times your site was visited during the selected period.

- ▶ **Pageviews.** The total number of times your site's pages were viewed during the selected period.

- ▶ **Pages/Visit.** The average number of pages viewed per visit.

- ▶ **Bounce Rate.** The percentage of visits in which the visitor doesn't stick around—that is, the visitor leaves your site after viewing just one page. Obviously, a high bounce rate means that people aren't inspired to more deeply explore your site; there may be something unappealing or not necessarily useful about the page they landed on.

- ▶ **Avg. Time on Site.** The average amount of time (in minutes and seconds) that a visit lasts on your site.

- ▶ **% New Visits.** The percent of visits from visitors who are new to your site.

You can display a full-page report for any of these metrics by clicking the item in the Site Usage table. For example, Figure 4.5 shows a full-page Bounce Rate report, with the bounce rate detailed on a daily basis.

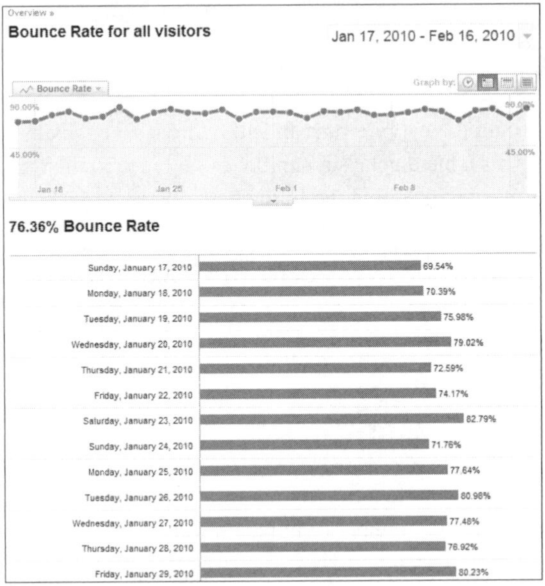

FIGURE 4.5   A full-page Bounce Rate report.

Visitors Overview

The Visitors Overview section, shown in Figure 4.6, displays a graph of the total number of visitors per day to your site. Click the View Report

FIGURE 4.6   The Visitors Overview section.

link to view more detailed visitor information, shown in Figure 4.7, including total visits, absolute unique visitors, pageviews, average pageviews, time on site, bounce rate, and new visits—as well as links to technical information about the browsers used and the visitors' connection speeds.

FIGURE 4.7   Displaying more detailed visitor information.

Map Overlay

The Map Overlay section, shown in Figure 4.8, displays a map of the world with countries highlighted that provided the most visitors to your site. Click the View Report link to view more detailed information by country, as shown in Figure 4.9.

Traffic Sources Overview

The Traffic Sources Overview section, shown in Figure 4.10, displays a pie chart that categorizes where your site's visits came from. Click the

FIGURE 4.8   The Map Overlay section.

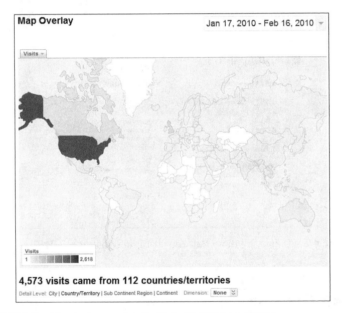

FIGURE 4.9   Viewing more detailed information by country.

View Report link to view this data in more detail, including the specific search engines that drove traffic, as well as the keywords searched that brought up your site in their results.

FIGURE 4.10   The Traffic Sources Overview section.

Content Overview

The Content Overview section, shown in Figure 4.11, is a list of the most-viewed pages on your site. Click the View Report link for more detailed data about your site's content—including links to a navigation analysis and a display of visitor click patterns for your page.

Content Overview		
Pages	Pagevi...	% Pageviews
/hobbies1.htm	1,030	12.83%
/drum_pictures.htm	996	12.41%
/tuning1.htm	727	9.06%
/	527	6.56%
/composing.htm	525	6.54%
view report		

FIGURE 4.11   The Content Overview section.

Sidebar

As useful as the Dashboard is, Google Analytics offers additional, more targeted reporting. You access this additional data from the sidebar on the left side of the page, as shown in Figure 4.12.

The major reporting types accessible from the sidebar include the following:

> ▶ **Intelligence.** Google Analytics Intelligence displays various automatic and custom alerts. Automatic alerts are generated when

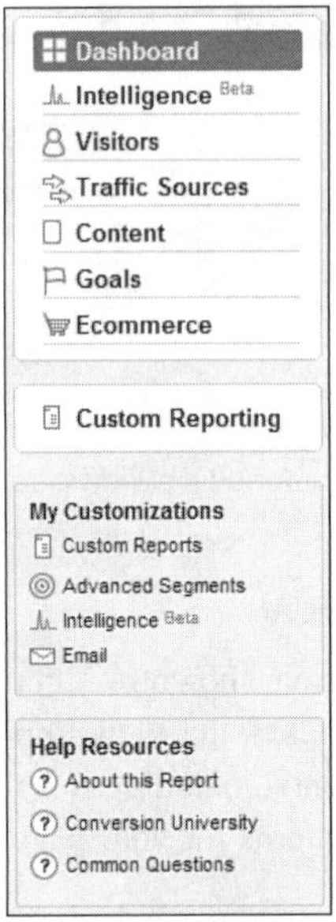

FIGURE 4.12   The Dashboard sidebar.

your site's actual performance differs significantly from expected performance; custom alerts are those you create to be notified when a certain performance threshhold is achieved.

▶ **Visitors.** These reports track various metrics related to your site's visitors. Available reports include Overview, Benchmarking, Map Overlay, New vs. Returning, Languages, Visitor Trending, Visitor Loyalty, Browser Capabilities, Network Properties, User Defined, and Custom Variables.

▶ **Traffic Sources.** These reports track the various sources of traffic to your site. Available reports include Overview, Direct Traffic, Referring Sites, Search Engines, All Traffic Sources, AdWords (if you're an advertiser), Keywords, Campaigns, and Ad Versions.

▶ **Content.** These reports track the pages and content on your site. Available reports include Overview, Top Content, Content by Title, Content Drilldown, Top Landing Pages, Top Exit Pages, and Site Overlay. There are additional reports for Site Search, AdSense, and Event Tracking.

▶ **Goals.** Do you have a defined goal for your site, in terms of visitors or sales or whatever? If so, you can set up those goals within Google Analytics and then track them with these reports: Overview, Total Conversions, Conversion Rate, Goal Abandoned Funnels, Goal Value, and Funnel Visualization.

▶ **Custom Reporting.** If none of these stock reports are to your liking, Google Analytics also lets you create all manner of custom reports. Click the Custom Reporting link to create any type of report you might need.

Exporting and Emailing Dashboard Data

If you want to view your site data offline, while you're not connected to the Google Analytics site, you can download the Dashboard page in either PDF or XML format. You can also email the Dashboard data to yourself or to any others you specify.

Exporting PDF Data

To download a copy of the Dashboard page as a PDF file, follow these steps:

1. From the Dashboard, click the Export button above the overview graph.

2. When the panel expands, as shown in Figure 4.13, click PDF.

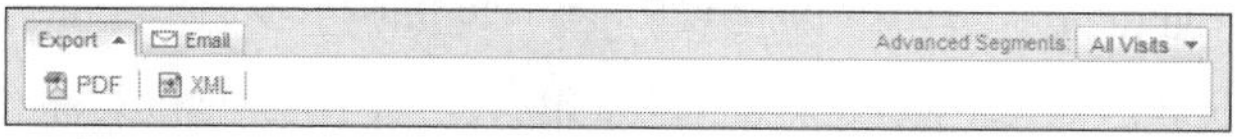

FIGURE 4.13   Exporting Dashboard data.

3. When the Save As dialog box appears, select a location for the PDF file and click Save.

Exporting XML Data

To download a copy of the Dashboard page as an XML file, follow these steps:

1. From the Dashboard, click the Export button above the overview graph.

2. When the panel expands, click XML.

3. When the Save As dialog box appears, select a location for the XML file and click Save.

Emailing PDF Data

You can also share your Dashboard data with others, via email. To email a copy of the Dashboard page, as a file attached to an email message, follow these steps:

1. From the Dashboard, click the Email button above the overview graph.

2. When the Set Up Email page appears, as shown in Figure 4.14, select the Send Now tab.

3. Enter the recipients' email addresses into the Send to Others box. Use commas to separate multiple addresses.

4. If you want a copy of the email sent to you, check the Send To Me option.

5. Enter a subject for the email message into the Subject box.

6. Enter a message for the email message into the Description box.

7. In the Format section, select the file format you want to send: PDF, XML, CSV, CSV for Excel, or TSV.

8. Enter the "secret word" into the Word Verification box.

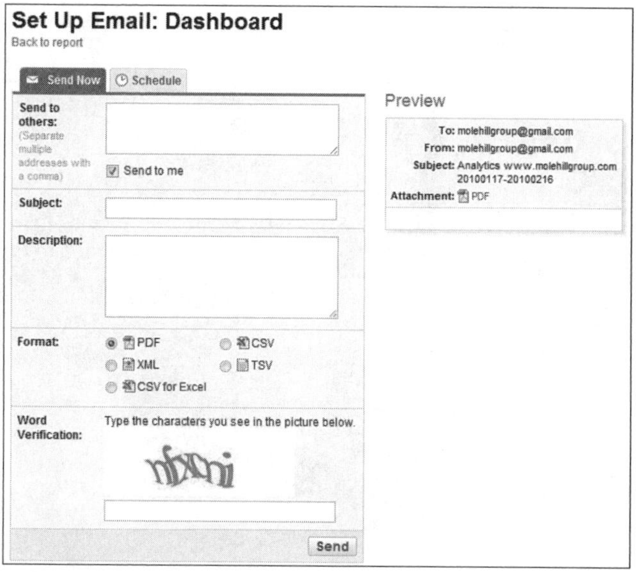

FIGURE 4.14   Sharing Dashboard data via email.

9. Click the Send button.

Google now sends an email message to the recipients you listed, with the Dashboard data attached to the message.

Summary

In this lesson, you learned how to navigate the Google Analytics Dashboard. In the next lesson, you learn how to customize the data displayed in the Dashboard.

LESSON 5

Customizing Data in the Dashboard

In this lesson, you learn how to customize the data displayed in the Dashboard's overview graph.

Displaying Different Metrics

The overview graph in the Google Analytics Dashboard is a useful tool for viewing essential information about your site's performance. It's also a versatile tool; although it displays visits per day by default, as shown in Figure 5.1, it can also graph other important metrics in a number of different ways.

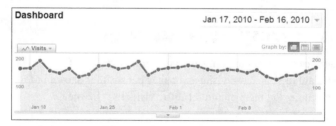

FIGURE 5.1 The overview graph on the Google Analytics Dashboard.

You can display the following metrics in the overview graph:

- ▶ Visits (default)
- ▶ Pageviews
- ▶ Pages/Visit

▶ Average Time on Site

▶ Bounce Rate

▶ % New Visits

To change the metric displayed in the graph, follow these steps:

1. Click the tab at the top of the overview graph.

2. This displays the Graph Mode pane, shown in Figure 5.2. Select one of the available metrics.

3. Click the tab again to hide the Graph Mode pane.

FIGURE 5.2   Selecting a metric from the Graph Mode pane.

Comparing Two Metrics

Sometimes it's useful to compare two different metrics. For example, you might want to show both visits and pages per visit, as shown in Figure 5.3, to get a more complete picture of those visits to your site.

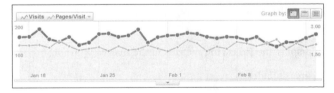

FIGURE 5.3   Comparing two metrics on the same graph.

To display two metrics on the same graph, follow these steps:

1. Click the tab at the top of the overview graph.

2. When the Graph Mode pane appears, click the Compare Two Metrics option.

3. This changes the pane to display a two-column list of available metrics, as shown in Figure 5.4. Select one metric from the left (blue) column and another from the right (orange).

FIGURE 5.4   Selecting two metrics to graph.

4. Click the tab again to hide the Graph Mode pane.

The first metric you selected, from the left column, displays as a blue line on the graph. The second metric you selected, from the right column, displays as an orange line on the graph.

Graphing by Day, Week, or Month

By default, the graph displays one data point for each day of the selected timeframe. You can, however, change this so that the graph displays one data point per week or per month. This is useful if you're graphing data for a long timeframe—several months, perhaps.

To change the data point display, click either the Day, Week, or Month button in the Graph By section at the top right of the graph, shown in Figure 5.5.

FIGURE 5.5   Selecting whether a single data point displays a day, week, or month's worth of data.

Changing the Date Range

By default, the overview graph displays data for the past month. You can, however, change the date range displayed on the graph. Follow these steps:

1. Click the down arrow next to the date range at the top right of the overview graph.

2. This expands the Date Range pane, as shown in Figure 5.6. Select the Calendar tab.

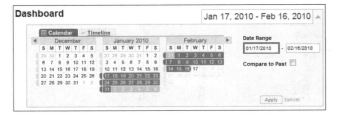

FIGURE 5.6   Selecting the range of dates to display from the Date Range pane.

3. There are several ways to select a date range. The first way is to click the first date of the range on the calendar and then click the last date in the range. This selects all dates in between the two selected dates.

4. The second way to select a date range is to enter the first and last dates into the Date Range boxes.

5. You can also select the Timeline tab, shown in Figure 5.7, and drag the left and right handles to select a given date range.

6. When you've selected the desired date range, click the Apply button.

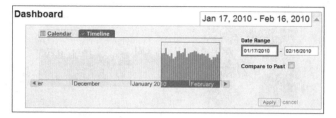

FIGURE 5.7   Selecting a date range from the Timeline tab in the Date Range pane.

Comparing Two Different Date Ranges

Another useful option is to display data from two different date ranges. You can, for example, display the average time on site data for the current month and the previous month, as shown in Figure 5.8. This lets you compare performance over two similar periods.

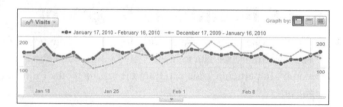

FIGURE 5.8   Comparing data from two different date ranges.

To compare data for two different date ranges, follow these steps:

1. Click the down arrow next to the date range at the top right of the overview graph.

2. When the Date Range pane appears, select the Calendar tab.

3. Click the Compare to Past option; this changes the pane, as shown in Figure 5.9.

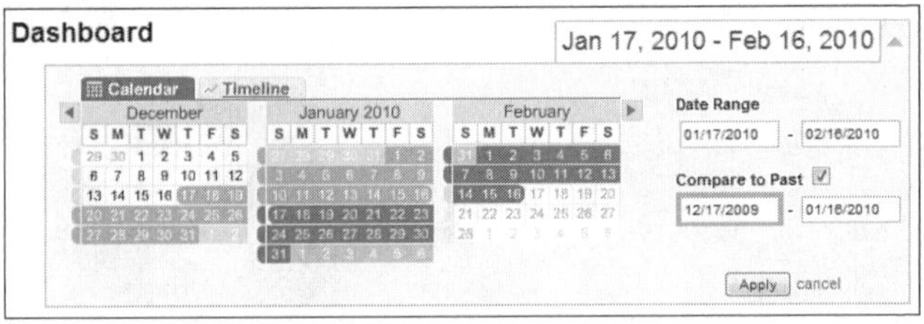

FIGURE 5.9   Comparing to past data.

4. Enter the first date range you want to compare into the Date Range boxes.

5. Enter the second date range you want to compare into the Compare to Past boxes.

6. Click the Apply button.

Filtering Results by Segment

By default, the overview graph displays data for all visitors to your site. You can, however, filter this data to display only information about certain types of visitors. In particular, you can filter the results by the following visitor segments:

▶ All Visits (default)

▶ New Visitors (people who haven't been to your site before)

▶ Returning Visitors (people who have been to your site before)

▶ Paid Search Traffic (traffic from AdWords and other PPC advertisements)

▶ Non-Paid Search Traffic (traffic from organic search results, such as Google search)

▶ Search Traffic (traffic from both organic and paid search)

▶ Direct Traffic (visitors who entered your URL directly—that is, they didn't click from another site)

▶ Referral Traffic (visitors who clicked a link to your site on another website)

▶ Visits with Conversions (if you're tracking conversions of visits into sales or some other goal, those visits that resulted in conversions)

▶ Visits from iPhones (visits from people viewing your site on their iPhones)

▶ Non-Bounce Visits (visits where people visited more than one page on your site)

To filter your results by visitor segment, follow these steps:

1. Click the button in the Advanced Segments section at the top-right corner above the overview graph.

2. This displays the Advanced Segments pane, shown in Figure 5.10. Select one or more visitor segments to display from the Default Segments list.

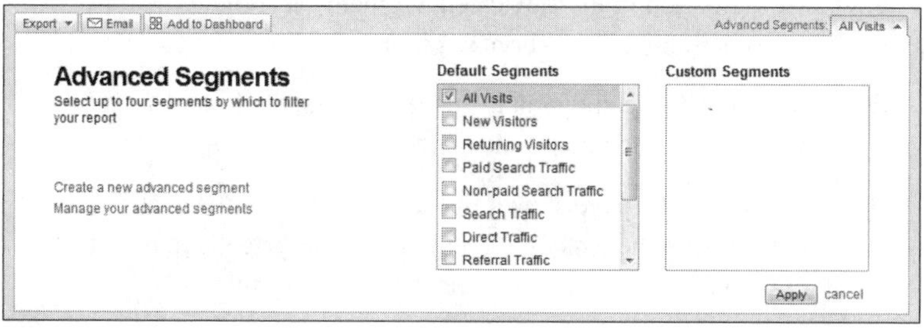

FIGURE 5.10   Filtering data by visitor segment.

3. Click the Apply button.

The overview graph will now display data only for those visitor segments you selected.

Creating Custom Visitor Segments

You're not limited to filtering your data by the dozen or so default visitor segments. You can also create your own custom visitor segments.

For example, you might want to display only those people who have viewed more than one page on your site. To do so, you create a statement like this:

Page Depth is greater than or equal to 2

You can even create complex statements to segment your visitors, using AND and OR Boolean operators. For example, you could create a visitor segment for new visitors who spent more than five minutes viewing each page. To do so, you create a statement that contains two arguments joined by an AND operator, like this:

Visitor Type matches exactly New Visitor AND Time on Page is greater than 5

It's all a matter of constructing a statement that defines a particular visitor segment. Follow these steps:

1. Click the button in the Advanced Segments section at the top-right corner above the overview graph.

2. When the Advanced Segments pane appears, click the Create a New Advanced Segment link.

3. You now see the page shown in Figure 5.11. Select a dimension or metric from the lists on the left side of the page, and drag that item onto the Dimension or Metric box on the right.

NOTE: **Dimensions and Metrics**

In Google Analytics parlance, a *dimension* is a visitor or campaign attribute. A *metric* is one of the values you select for your report. Dimensions are typically text, whereas metrics are typically numbers.

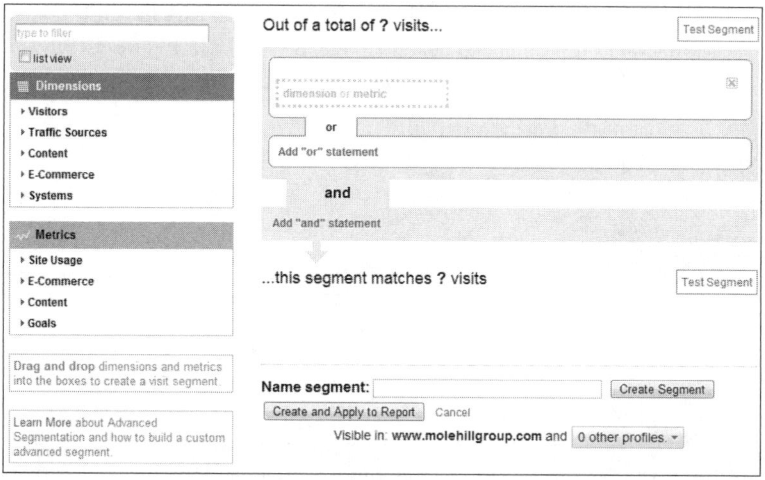

FIGURE 5.11   Crafting a statement to define a new visitor segment.

4. This now expands this section of the page, as shown in Figure 5.12. Pull down the Condition list and select a condition statement (Matches Exactly, Does Not Match Exactly, Contains, Does Not Contain, and so on).

5. Enter a value for the dimension or metric into the Value box, or select from the pull-down menu, to complete the display statement.

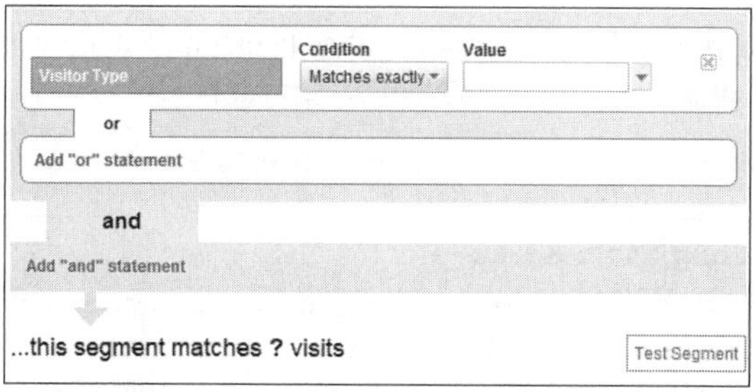

FIGURE 5.12   Adding a condition and value to the statement.

6. To add an OR argument to the statement, click the Add "Or" Statement link; this expands the page, as shown in Figure 5.13.

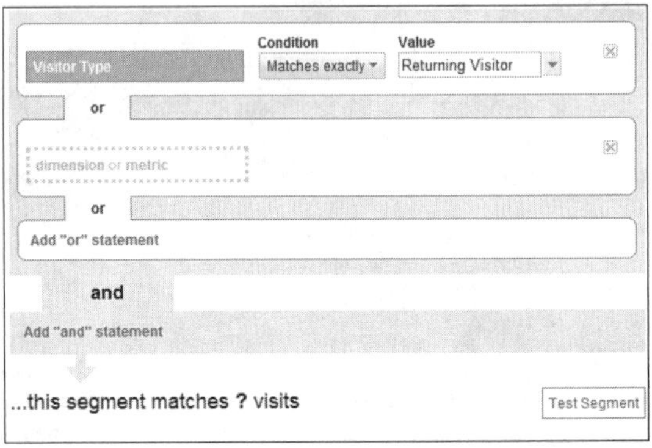

FIGURE 5.13   Adding an OR argument to the statement.

Construct this new statement by repeating the instructions in Steps 3–5.

7. To add an AND argument to the statement, click the Add "And" Statement link; then construct this new statement by repeating the instructions in Steps 3–5.

NOTE: **Deleting Statements**
To delete any part of a statement, click the X box for that part of the statement.

8. When you're done constructing the statement, enter a name for this new segment into the Name Segment box.

9. Click the Create and Apply to Report button.

NOTE: **Testing Statements**
To test the statement you're constructing—that is, to see if it actually generates data—click the Test Segment button.

Annotating Data Points

There's one last thing you can do with the overview graph: annotate individual data points. For example, you might have a single day where site traffic jumped considerably; you could add an annotation to this day's data point to explain the jump in traffic. Annotations can be seen by anyone with access to a Google Analytics profile.

To add a data point annotation, follow these steps:

1. On the overview graph, click the data point you want to annotate.

2. This displays the pop-up box shown in Figure 5.14. Click Create New Annotation.

FIGURE 5.14   The pop-up box for a selected data point.

3. This expands the Annotation pane below the graph, as shown in Figure 5.15. Enter the text for the annotation into the text box. (Annotations can be up to 160 characters long.)

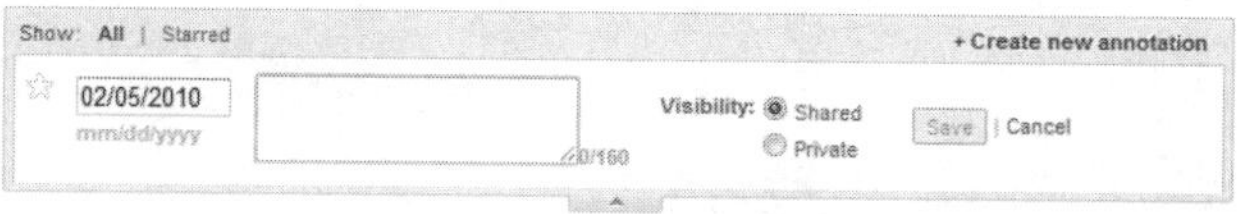

FIGURE 5.15   Adding an annotation in the Annotation pane.

4. Click the Save button.

To view annotations on the graph, click the Show All link beneath the graph. This lists all annotations you've created, as shown in Figure 5.16; click the annotation in the list to highlight the data point on the graph.

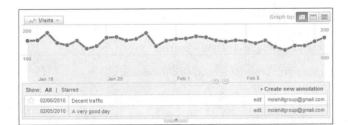

FIGURE 5.16   Displaying all annotations.

> **NOTE: Starred Annotations**
> To highlight special annotations, click the star icon next to the annotation. You can then display only starred annotations by clicking Show Starred beneath the graph.

Summary

In this lesson, you learned how to sort and filter data in the Dashboard's overview graph. In the next lesson, you learn how to track visitors to your site.

LESSON 6

Tracking Visitors

In this lesson, you learn how to track the visitors to your site.

Understanding Visitor Tracking

When it comes to website visitors, quality is just as important as quantity. Yes, it matters how many visitors you get, but it also matters where they come from, how long they stay, and whether they return or not.

To that end, most serious webmasters collect a lot of data about the visitors to their websites. This data is available from Google Analytics, and you can slice it and dice it in a variety of different ways.

The most basic visitor data is the raw count of site visits—how many times your site was viewed in a given time period. This one is simple to understand; the more visits you get, the better.

Visits do not equal visitors, however, as a single visitor can make more than one visit. For that reason, you need to track the unique visitors to your site.

You should also track new and repeat visitors separately; you want a good mix of new and repeating traffic to your site. A mix that leans toward new visitors indicates your site is not doing a good job of retaining previous visitors. Conversely, a site that leans toward repeat visitors isn't doing a good-enough job attracting new traffic.

How long visitors stay on your site is predictive of how many repeat visitors you'll get. To that end, take a good look at the time on site and bounce rate metrics. The longer your visitors spend on your site, the more value they're finding. Conversely, if you have a high bounce rate—the percentage of visits from visitors who leave without viewing a second page—then you're not providing enough value in your content to keep them sticking around.

Of course, there are other visitor metrics you can track. When you're designing your pages, it helps to know your visitors' technical capabilities—what screen resolution they use, what browsers they use, whether they have Flash and Java installed, that sort of thing. Some webmasters like to know what ISPs and domains are driving traffic to their sites. And it's always interesting to know where your visitors live and what languages they speak.

All this data, and more, is available in the Visitors section of Google Analytics. There are more than a dozen different reports available, all providing practical analysis of the people who visit your website.

Viewing the Visitors Overview

When you want to learn more about the visitors to your site, the best place to start is with the Visitors Overview report, shown in Figure 6.1. To display the Visitors Overview report, select Visitors > Overview from the navigation pane of the Google Analytics Dashboard.

The Visitors Overview report displays the following essential information about your site's visitors:

▶ **Overview graph.** By default, this displays visitors per day for the past month. Like the identical overview graph on the Dashboard, however, you can configure the graph to track other metrics over different timeframes.

▶ **Visits.** The number of times your site was visited during the selected period.

TIP: **Detailed Reports**
To display more detailed information for any of the key metrics displayed on the Visitors Overview page, simply click the metric name. For example, to display a day-by-day report of visits, click the pageviews metric.

FIGURE 6.1 The Visitors Overview report.

▶ **Absolute Unique Visitors.** The number of unique visitors to your site during the selected time period.

▶ **Pageviews.** The number of individual pages viewed during the selected time period.

▶ **Average Pageviews.** The average number of pageviews per visit during the selected time period.

▶ **Time on Site.** The average amount of time, in minutes and seconds, that a typical visit lasted on your site during the selected time period.

▶ **Bounce Rate.** The percent of visits from visitors who visited just one page on your site before leaving to visit another site.

▶ **New Visits.** The percent of total visits that were from new visitors to your site.

▶ **Technical Profile.** This table at the bottom of the page, shown in Figure 6.2, displays technical information about your site's visitors. In particular, you see how many visits were made by users of the most popular web browsers (Internet Explorer, Firefox, Safari, Google Chrome, and Opera), as well as how many visits were made via various Internet connection speeds (cable, DSL, T1, and dialup).

Technical Profile

Browser	Visits	% visits	Connection Speed	Visits	% visits
Internet Explorer	2,398	52.44%	Cable	1,621	35.45%
Firefox	1,373	30.02%	Unknown	1,172	25.63%
Safari	404	8.83%	DSL	1,162	25.41%
Chrome	242	5.29%	T1	460	10.06%
Opera	70	1.53%	Dialup	123	2.69%
view full report			view full report		

FIGURE 6.2 The Technical Profile section of the Visitors Overview page.

▶ **Visitor Segmentation.** This section of the Visitors Overview page links to reports that segment your site's visits by a number of variables; click any variable to display the full report. You can track visitors by their visitor profiles (languages and network locations/service providers), their browser profiles (browser, operating system, number of screen colors, screen resolution, Java support, and Flash support), and their geographical location (via a map overlay). For example, Figure 6.3 displays the Service Providers report, which you display by clicking the Network Locations link; this report tells you how many of your visits come from visitors who subscribe to particular Internet Service Providers (ISPs).

Benchmarking Visitor Statistics

Viewing your site's visitor statistics in a vacuum doesn't tell you a whole lot about how your site is performing vis-à-vis similar sites. To get more of

FIGURE 6.3   Tracking visitors by Internet Service Provider.

a performance comparison, you need to *benchmark* your site against indus-try-wide statistics.

NOTE: **Enabling Benchmarking**

Before you can display the visitor benchmarking report, you need to enable benchmarking for your site. To do this, go to the Google Analytics Overview page and click the Edit Account Settings link. When the Edit Analytics Account page appears, scroll to the Google Analytics Data Sharing Settings section and select the Share My Google Analytics Data Anonymously with Google and Others setting; then click the Save Settings button.

To display the Benchmarking report, select Visitors > Benchmarking from the left panel. As you can see in Figure 6.4, this page displays six graphs that compare visitor data from your site with data from other sites of a similar size. The data compared include the following:

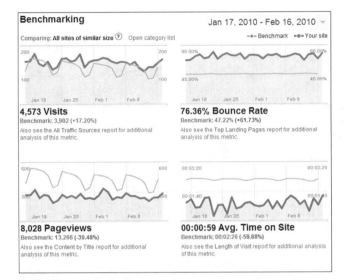

FIGURE 6.4　Comparing the performance of your site with similar sites.

▶ Visits

▶ Bounce Rate

▶ Pageviews

▶ Avg. Time on Site

▶ Pages/Visit

▶ New Visits

Each of these graphs displays data from your site in blue, and industry data in orange. The average for your site and the industry benchmark is displayed beneath each graph, along with the percentage difference between the two. It's a good way to determine if you're doing better or worse than similar and competing websites.

> NOTE: **Category Selection**
>
> By default, Google Analytics benchmarks your site against other sites of a similar size. To benchmark against sites (of all sizes) in a

given category, click the Open Category list link, select a category from the list, and then click the Select Category button.

Mapping Visitors by Region

Visitors to your site can be located anywhere in the world. Google Analytics lets you track visitors by where they live, via a graphic map, like the one shown in Figure 6.5. To display the Map Overlay, select Visitors > Map Overlay from the left side panel on the Dashboard.

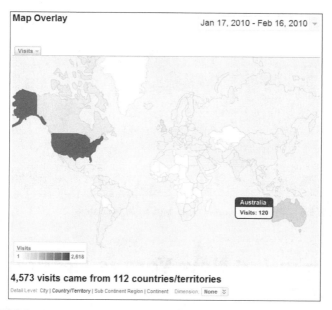

Map Overlay   Jan 17, 2010 - Feb 16, 2010

Visits

Australia
Visits: 120

Visits
1   2,618

4,573 visits came from 112 countries/territories
Detail Level: City | Country/Territory | Sub Continent Region | Continent   Dimension: None

FIGURE 6.5   Viewing the Map Overlay page.

Those countries that are host to the most visits appear in darker shades of green; those countries with fewer visits appear in lighter shades of green; those counties with no visits appear in white.

Beneath the map is a table that lists the most popular countries of origin in descending order. For each country, you can see the total number of visits, pages per visit, average time on site, percent new visits, and bounce rate.

By default, this page displays country-level detail. However, you can also display city-, sub-continent-, and continent-level detail by clicking the appropriate link underneath the map. For example, Figure 6.6 shows the Map Overlay displaying city-level detail; each dot on the map represents a major city, which are detailed in the table below the map.

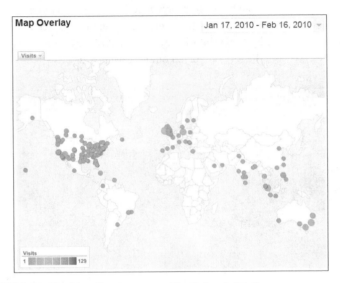

FIGURE 6.6   The Map Overlay page with city-level detail.

Comparing New Versus Returning Visitors

Most websites want to foster a healthy mix of new visitors and returning visitors. New visitors help increase a site's audience and visitation over time, whereas repeat visitors are an indication of the value and freshness of the site's content.

You can compare the mix of new vs. returning visitors by selecting Visitors > New vs. Returning from the left side panel on the Dashboard. This displays the New vs. Returning page, shown in Figure 6.7. The

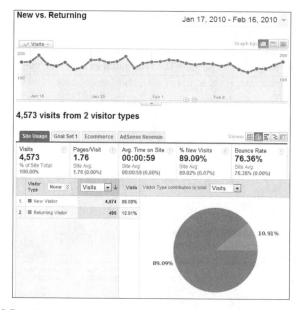

FIGURE 6.7   New and returning visitors compared, via a pie chart.

valuable data on this page is not in the top graph, which is a rehash of the Dashboard's overview graph. Instead, the bottom of the page displays a pie chart that shows the percentage of new (blue) and returning (green) visitors. The percentages are also detailed in the accompanying table.

> **NOTE: Additional Data**
>
> You can also display other data for new and returning visitor types. Pull down the list in the table or above the pie chart to select Visits, Pageviews, Time on Site, New Visits, or Bounces.

Viewing Visitors by Language

If knowing what countries your visitors come from is useful, it's often equally useful to know what languages they speak—so you can design the content of your site accordingly. You can view your visitors' language mix (as determined by their web browser settings) by selecting Visitors > Languages from the left side panel on the Dashboard.

The Languages page, shown in Figure 6.8, displays the typical overview graph at the top but a more relevant language list at the bottom. The languages used by your visitors are listed in descending order of frequency; for each language listed, you see the total number of visits, pages per visit, average time on site, percent new visits, and bounce rate.

FIGURE 6.8   Viewing the languages used by your site's visitors.

Analyzing Visitor Trends

When you're analyzing your site's performance, it's important to look at how various metrics change over time. Are you getting more visitors or fewer? Do your pages have a higher bounce rate or a lower one? Are visitors spending more time per visit or less?

Fortunately, Google Analytics makes it easy to look at all sorts of visitor trends. When you select Visitors > Visitor Trending in the left side panel of the Dashboard, you now have six new reports you can view. These reports show you how key metrics change over time, and include the following:

- ▶ Visits

- ▶ Absolute Unique Visitors

- ▶ Pageviews

- ▶ Average Pageviews

- ▶ Time on Site

- ▶ Bounce Rate

As an example, Figure 6.9 shows the Average Pageviews report. The graph at the top of the page tracks average pageviews for each day during the past month; the table below the graph displays the raw numbers per day.

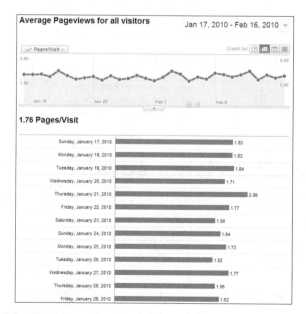

FIGURE 6.9 The Average Pageviews visitor trends report.

What's unique about the visitor trends reports is that you have an option to graph the data by hour, in addition to the normal day, week, and month options. Click the Hour button in the Graph By section, shown in Figure 6.10, and you now see how the selected metric trends during each part of the day. You might be surprised to see how differently your site is used over the course of a 24-hour period.

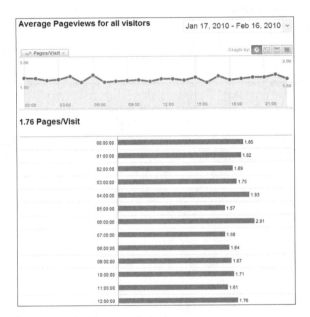

FIGURE 6.10   Viewing visitor trends by hour.

Analyzing Visitor Loyalty

How loyal are your site's visitors? That is, how often do the same people repeatedly visit your site?

You can track visitor loyalty by selecting Visitors > Visitor Loyalty from the left panel of the Dashboard. From here, you can display four different reports:

▶ **Loyalty**, shown in Figure 6.11, which tracks how many times visitors have seen your site. That is, you see how many visitors have visited your site one time in the select period, two times, three times, and so forth.

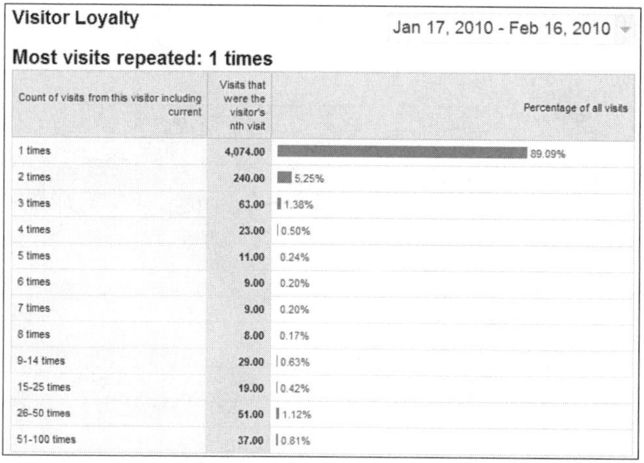

Visitor Loyalty		Jan 17, 2010 - Feb 16, 2010 ▾
Most visits repeated: 1 times		

Count of visits from this visitor including current	Visits that were the visitor's nth visit	Percentage of all visits
1 times	4,074.00	89.09%
2 times	240.00	5.25%
3 times	63.00	1.38%
4 times	23.00	0.50%
5 times	11.00	0.24%
6 times	9.00	0.20%
7 times	9.00	0.20%
8 times	8.00	0.17%
9-14 times	29.00	0.63%
15-25 times	19.00	0.42%
26-50 times	51.00	1.12%
51-100 times	37.00	0.81%

FIGURE 6.11   Analyzing visitor loyalty.

▶ **Recency**, which tells you when visitors had their previous visit— 1 day ago, 2 days ago, and so forth.

▶ **Length of Visit**, which tells you how long visitors spent on your site. Longer visits are normally better.

▶ **Depth of Visit**, which tells you how many pageviews each visitor had. Obviously, the more pages visited, the more in-depth the visitor experience.

Viewing Visitors' Browser Capabilities

If you want to make sure your site looks best for all your users, you can examine what types of browsers, operating systems, and the like are used by your visitors. You do this by selecting Visitors > Browser Capabilities from the left panel on the Dashboard. From here you can display the following technical reports:

▶ **Browsers**, shown in Figure 6.12, which analyzes which web browsers your visitors are using.

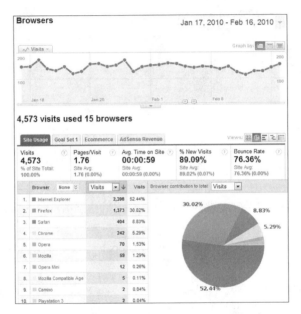

FIGURE 6.12   Examining which web browsers are used to view your site.

▶ **Operating Systems**, which tracks the operating systems used by your visitors.

▶ **Browsers and OS**, which shows you which browser/operating system combinations are employed by your visitors.

▶ **Screen Colors**, which displays the bit depth (32-bit, 24-bit, and so on) of the displays in your visitors' computer systems.

▶ **Screen Resolution**, which lists the resolution of your visitors' displays.

▶ **Flash Versions**, which tracks which versions of the Adobe Flash plug-in your visitors have installed.

▶ **Java Support**, which examines whether or not your visitors have Java enabled in their browsers.

Viewing Visitors' Network Properties

Some webmasters may be interested in the more technical aspects of their site's visitors—which ISPs they use, which hosts drive the most traffic, and at what speeds their visitors connect. These data are available when you select Visitors > Network Properties from the left panel of the Dashboard. There are three reports available here:

▶ **Service Providers**, shown in Figure 6.13, which tracks your visitors' ISPs.

FIGURE 6.13 Viewing information about your visitors' Internet service providers.

▶ **Host Names**, which tracks the domain hosts of your site visitors.

▶ **Connection Speeds**, which tracks the speeds of your visitors' connections—cable, DSL, T1, ISDN, dialup, and so forth.

Viewing Mobile Visitors

These days, a computer isn't the only way to surf the web. More and more users are browsing the Internet from their iPhones, Nexus Ones, and other smartphones.

If you want to learn more about mobile visitors to your site, select Visitors > Mobile from the left panel of the Dashboard. You now have two reports to choose from:

▶ **Mobile Devices**, shown in Figure 6.14, which tracks mobile visitors by the kind of device they use.

▶ **Mobile Carriers**, which tracks mobile visitors by their mobile service.

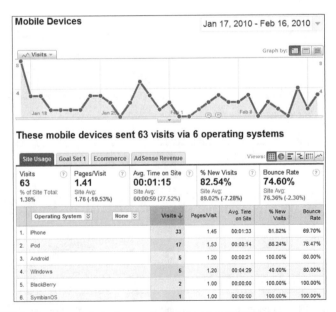

FIGURE 6.14   Examining site usage by type of mobile device.

Summary

In this lesson, you learned a number of ways to track the visitors to your website. In the next lesson, you learn how to analyze your site's traffic sources.

LESSON 7

Analyzing Traffic Sources

In this lesson, you learn how to analyze the sources of traffic to your website.

Where Does Your Traffic Come From?

In the previous lesson, we examined ways to analyze the visitors to your site. Equally important, though, is where these visitors come from—that is, how they're finding your site.

In general, there are four ways for a new visitor to come to your site, as follows:

- ▶ **Directly,** by entering your site's URL into their web browser or using a browser bookmark.

- ▶ **Referral,** by clicking a link to your site found on another site.

- ▶ **Search engine,** by searching for a keyword and finding your website in the search results.

- ▶ **Campaigns,** by clicking on an advertisement you've purchased for your site, such as AdWords, or on a link in an email newsletter.

Which of these methods is best? There's no hard and fast answer to that question, although most sites get the majority of their new visitors from Google and other search engines. It's healthy, however, to also get a fair number of new visitors from links on referring sites. And there's nothing wrong with buying new visitors via pay-per-click (PPC) advertising. One wouldn't expect, however, to find too many new visitors who already know your URL and enter it directly.

Google Analytics tracks the last site your visitors visited before they came to your site. And, when it comes to traffic sourced from search engines, you can also learn what queries these users made that generated your site in their search results.

Viewing the Traffic Sources Overview

To gain an overview of the source of traffic to your website, access the Traffic Sources Overview report, shown in Figure 7.1. You view this report by selecting Traffic Sources > Overview in the left pane of the Google Analytics Dashboard.

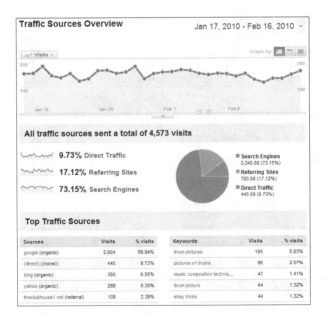

FIGURE 7.1   Viewing the Traffic Sources Overview report.

The top of this report displays the ubiquitous overview graph, so you can just ignore that. Instead, focus on the data table and pie chart directly beneath the graph; it's here where you see what percent of site visits came from direct traffic, referring sites, and search engines. (Or, if you've advertised your site via ad campaigns, which percent came from those campaigns.)

Scroll down further to the Top Traffic Sources lists, and you can see the top individual sources of traffic to your site. This list may include the major search engines (Google, Yahoo!, and Bing), direct visits, as well as any sites that link to your site.

Click the View Full Report link to view a more complete All Traffic Sources report, like the one shown in Figure 7.2. This report displays the top traffic sources in descending order, along with the number of visits, pages per visit, average time on site, percent new visits, and bounce rate associated with each source.

FIGURE 7.2   The full All Traffic Sources report.

Also in the Top Traffic Sources report are the top keywords and key phrases searched for by users who found your site on Google and other search engines. Google Analytics displays the number of visits resulting from each keyword search, as well as what percent of your site's total visits was associated with each keyword.

> NOTE: **Keywords**
> A *keyword* is a word or phrase included in a search query.

Click the View Full Report link to view a more complete list of keywords used, like the one shown in Figure 7.3. This report lists the most searched-for keywords in descending order, along with the number of visits, pages per visit, average time on site, percent new visits, and bounce rate associated with each keyword.

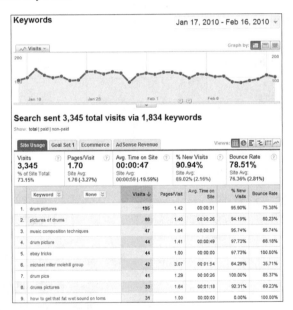

FIGURE 7.3   The full Keywords report.

> NOTE: **Keywords Report**
> You can also display the Keywords report by selecting Traffic Sources > Keywords from the left pane of the Dashboard.

Analyzing Direct Traffic

Google Analytics also lets you analyze traffic from each type of source individually. We'll start by looking at direct traffic—those visitors who come to your site by entering your site's URL into their web browsers or by selecting a bookmark.

You display the Direct Traffic report, shown in Figure 7.4, by selecting Traffic Sources > Direct Traffic from the left pane of the Dashboard. There's the ever-present overview graph at the top of the report, which in this instance displays visits per day for your site's direct traffic. Beneath that, you see a listing of statistics for your site's direct visitors. These statistics include the following:

FIGURE 7.4   The Direct Traffic report.

- ▶ **Visits** coming from direct traffic, as well as what percent of your total visits this represents.

- ▶ **Avg. Time on Site** from your direct visitors, compared to your site's overall average time on site.

- ▶ **Bounce Rate**, or what percentage of visitors leave after visiting only the first page. This is also compared to the overall bounce rate for your site.

▶ **Pages/Visit**, compared to your site's average pages/visit.

▶ **% New Visits**, or what percentage of this direct traffic consists of new visitors to your site. This is also compared with your site average.

NOTE: **Overview Graph**

To change the metric displayed in the overview graph, click the graph icon next to any of the metrics (Visits, Bounce Rate, and so forth) displayed at the bottom of the page.

Analyzing Traffic from Referring Sites

Any site that contains a link back to your site is a *referring site*, and visitors clicking on these links are *referred visitors*. To learn more about these referred visits, select Traffic Sources > Referring Sites from the left pane of the Dashboard.

This displays the Referring Sites report, shown in Figure 7.5. The overview graph at the top of this report displays the total number of referred visits per day, whereas the bottom of the page lists the most popular referring sites. Above this table are the statistics for these referring sites—visits, pages per visit, average time on site, percent new visits, and bounce rate. These same statistics are listed for each of the top referring sites.

By default, the Referring Sites report lists the top ten referring sites. To display the next ten referring sites (and the next ten after that, and so on), click the right arrow button beneath the list. To display more detailed information about any individual referring site, simply click its name in the list.

NOTE: **Displaying Detail**

If you'd prefer to display statistics about referring sites in the aggregate, instead of a site list, click the Detail button above the referring site list.

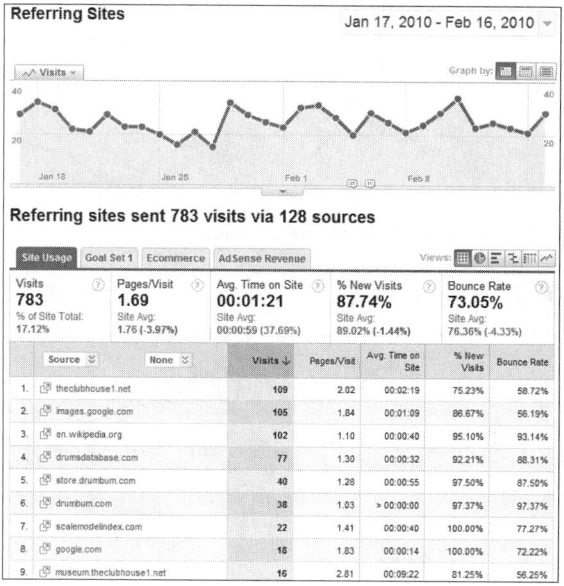

FIGURE 7.5 The Referring Sites report.

Analyzing Traffic from Search Engines

Most websites derive the majority of new visitors from the major search engines. That is, a person searches for a particular topic, generates a list of search results, and clicks your site within this list.

To that end, analyzing which search engines generate the most traffic, as well as which keywords led to your site, is quite useful. All this information is found in the Search Engines report, shown in Figure 7.6. You generate this report by selecting Traffic Sources > Search Engines from the left pane of the Dashboard.

The top of the Search Engines report displays the overview graph, which tracks visits per day for search engine traffic. Beneath that are the statistics for aggregate search engine traffic—visits, pages per visit, average time on site, percent new visits, and bounce rate. Beneath that is a list of search

FIGURE 7.6   The Search Engines report.

engines that drove the most traffic to your site, with the same statistics listed for each search engine.

To further analyze the traffic from each search engine, click a search engine's name in the list. This displays a report for that search engine, like the one shown in Figure 7.7. Beneath the overview report (which displays visits per day from that search engine), you find a list of the top ten keywords used to find your site on that search engine, along with statistics for each keyword. To view the next ten keywords (and the next and the next), click the right arrow beneath the list.

NOTE: **AdWords Traffic**

You can also drive traffic to your site with AdWords advertising. Learn more in Lesson 11, "Tracking AdWords Traffic."

FIGURE 7.7   A report for a specific search engine.

Summary

In this lesson, you learned how to examine the sources of traffic to your website. In the next lesson, you learn how to analyze the content of your website.

LESSON 8

Analyzing Top Content

In this lesson, you learn how to analyze the popularity of the content on your site.

Why Content Analysis Matters

The typical website consists of many, many individual pages. Some pages appeal to some types of users; other pages appeal to other users. Some pages do a good job of retaining visitors; others don't. Some pages just attract more traffic than do others.

When you want to optimize your site—to make each page as effective as possible—you need to know which pages are working and which aren't. This is where content analysis comes in.

Content analysis looks at each page of your site and determines which pages are pulling their weight and which aren't. There are lots of different metrics to look at, but in general, you want to know which pages attract the most visitors (these are your top *landing pages*—where people enter your site from other sites), as well as which pages people tend to leave from (these are the *exit pages*—where people decide they don't want to stick around any longer). You also want to know which pages are the most popular on your site, as measured in visitors and pageviews; these are the pages that obviously have the most appeal to visitors.

A page that has a large number of pageviews, or one that is a top landing page, likely is attracting visitors because of its content. The better the content—that is, the more useful, relevant, and unique the content—the more attractive it will be to visitors, whether they're coming from search engines or other sites. A page that doesn't have a lot of pageviews and isn't a big landing page destination is probably one with weak content, which you need to examine and revamp.

As such, you can use these content metrics to fine-tune your site's content. Identify the strong pages and work to make them even stronger; find the weak pages and either get rid of them or rework them. The goal is to have a site where almost every page offers unique value that attracts both new and repeat visitors.

Viewing the Content Overview Report

The key content metrics are found on the Content Overview report, shown in Figure 8.1. You access this report by selecting Content > Overview from the left pane in the Google Analytics Dashboard.

FIGURE 8.1   The Content Overview report.

Viewing the Overview Graph

At the top of the Content Overview report is the overview graph. This graph displays total pageviews per day for the past month. Like all overview graphs, you can configure it to display other metrics, by clicking the tab on the top left of the graph, as shown in Figure 8.2. The following metrics are available:

FIGURE 8.2   Viewing additional metrics in the overview graph.

▶ **Pageviews**, the number of total pages that have been displayed.

▶ **Unique Pageviews**, which reports the number of sessions during which pages have been viewed; a user viewing the same page twice in a session would generate a single pageview.

▶ **Avg. Time on Page**, measured in minutes and seconds.

▶ **Bounce Rate**, the percent of visits from visitors who exit without viewing a second page.

▶ **% Exit**, the percentage of views of a page that were the last page viewed during a visit.

▶ **$ Index**, displayed if you're a Google AdSense subscriber, which calculates the average value for a page a user visits before completing the desired transaction.

▶ **AdSense Revenue**, the amount of money generated from AdSense ads on your site.

▶ **AdSense Page Impressions**, the number of times an ad was displayed.

▶ **AdSense Ad Units Viewed**, the number of ads displayed.

Check the metric you want displayed; then click the tab again to redisplay the graph.

Viewing the Key Statistics

Beneath the overview graph is a list of three key content-oriented metrics: Pageviews, Unique Views, and Bounce Rate. Click the graph icon to the left of each item to display that metric in the overview graph. Click the link for each metric to display a more detailed report for that metric.

> NOTE: **AdSense**
>
> If you subscribe to Google's AdSense program to put PPC ads on your site, Google integrates AdSense reporting into its content reports. On the Content Overview page, this takes the form of an AdSense Performance section, which lists three key AdSense metrics: AdSense Page Impressions, AdSense Revenue, and AdSense Unit Impressions. Learn more about these and other related metrics in Lesson 9, "Tracking AdSense Peformance."

Viewing Top Content

Which are the most-viewed pages on your site? Your top five pages, in terms of pageviews, are listed in the Top Content section. View the next most-viewed pages by clicking the View Full Report link.

View more details about each page by clicking that page in the list. This displays the Content Detail report for that page, like the one shown in Figure 8.3. This report displays the following information for the selected page:

▶ Pageviews

▶ Unique Views

▶ Time on Page

▶ Bounce Rate

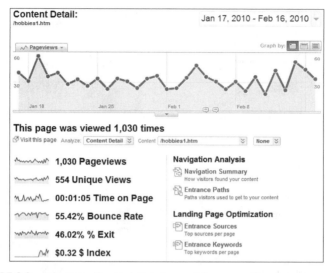

FIGURE 8.3   Viewing a Content Detail report for a specific page on your site.

▶ % Exit

▶ $ Index

If you're an AdSense subscriber, you'll also see three key AdSense metrics (AdSense Page Impressions, AdSense Revenue, and AdSense Unit Impressions).

Performing a Navigation Analysis

On the right side of the Content Overview page, beneath the overview graph, are two links that aid in your analysis of site navigation—how people get around your site.

Click the Navigation Summary link to display the Navigation Summary report, shown in Figure 8.4. Beneath the obligatory overview graph is a section that compares site entrances with site exits. This compares the percent of visits entering your site at a given page to those that exited your site on the same page. There is also a list of Previous Pages (those pages on your site that visitors viewed previous to visiting a page), as well as a list of Next Pages (those pages on your site that visitors went to after viewing the page).

Navigation Summary: Jan 17, 2010 - Feb 16, 2010

This page was viewed 527 times

78.29% Entrances   **21.85%** Exits

21.71% Previous Pages   **78.15%** Next Pages

Content	% Clicks
/ty-youtube.htm	2.30%
/win7yourway.htm	2.30%
/computer_basics.htm	1.88%
/easy_computer_ba...	1.67%
/percussion.htm	1.67%
/biblogr.htm	1.25%
/author.htm	1.04%
/internet.htm	1.04%
/index.html	0.84%
/digital_lifestyles.htm	0.84%

Content	% Clicks
/biblogr.htm	8.62%
/author.htm	6.77%
/computer_basics.htm	6.46%
/win7yourway.htm	5.54%
/music.htm	4.00%
/easy_computer_ba...	4.00%
/music_theory.htm	3.69%
/ty-youtube.htm	3.69%
/percussion.htm	3.69%
/index.html	3.38%

FIGURE 8.4   The Navigation Summary report.

Click the Entrance Paths link to display the Entrance Paths report, shown in Figure 8.5. This report displays those pages that visitors viewed after starting on a page; select one of the next pages in the middle column to view the final pages these visitors viewed during these visits.

> NOTE: **Entrance Paths**
> The Entrance Paths report is particularly useful in examining how typical users navigate your site—the paths they take while they're there.

Performing Landing Page Optimization

Beneath the Navigation Analysis section are links to two reports that help you analyze and optimize your landing pages—the pages on which visitors first land when they go to your site.

This page was viewed 527 times

Visit this page Analyze: [Entrance Paths] Content [/]

Started here	Then viewed these pages:			And ended up here:		
	Content	Visits	% visits	Content	Visits	% visits
This Page	/	30	13.70%	/bibliogr.htm	5	20.00%
	/bibliogr.htm	25	11.42%	/	4	16.00%
	/author.htm	19	8.68%	/cloud_computing.htm	3	12.00%
	/computer_basic...	16	7.31%	/theory-corrections.htm	3	12.00%
	/music_theory.htm	11	5.02%	/bookstor.htm	1	4.00%
	/music.htm	10	4.57%	/your_first_notebook_...	1	4.00%
	/win7yourway.htm	10	4.57%	/index.html	1	4.00%
	/easy_computer_...	10	4.57%	/author.htm	1	4.00%
	/internet.htm	9	4.11%	/badpics.htm	1	4.00%
	/digital_lifestyles...	8	3.65%	/default1.htm	1	4.00%
	Show rows: [10] 1 - 10 of 38			Show rows: [10] 1 - 10 of 14		

FIGURE 8.5   The Entrance Paths report.

Click the Entrance Sources link to display the Entrance Sources report, shown in Figure 8.6. This report lists those pages outside your site that visitors viewed just prior to displaying a page.

Click the Entrance Keywords link to display the Entrance Keywords report. This report lists the keywords that people searched for that led them to a given page on your site.

For either of these reports, you can analyze a page other than your home page by selecting a new page from the Content pull-down list. This list displays your top landing pages; it's entirely possible that you have more people entering your site at another page than at your home page.

> NOTE: **Site Overlay**
> The Content Overview page also includes a Click Patterns section, which generates a site overlay map. Learn more in Lesson 10, "Viewing the Site Overlay Report."

Viewing Your Top Pages

When it comes to examining the most-viewed pages on your site, you have two ways to do it. You can look at your top pages by URL or by page title.

FIGURE 8.6 The Entrance Sources report.

To display a list of your top pages by URL, select Content > Top Content in the left pane of the Dashboard. To display a list of your top pages by page title, select Content > Content by Title.

> **NOTE: Content Drilldown**
>
> If you have your site organized in a structure with folders and sub-folders, you can observe the performance of each subfolder by using the Content Drilldown report. Open this report by selecting Content > Content Drilldown.

In either case, the resulting report looks like the one in Figure 8.7, with your top ten pages listed in descending order. Click the right arrow under this list to display the next ten pages, then the next, then the next.

For each page listed, Google displays a variety of key metrics—Pageviews, Unique Pageviews, Avg. Time on Page, Bounce Rate, % Exit, and $ Index.

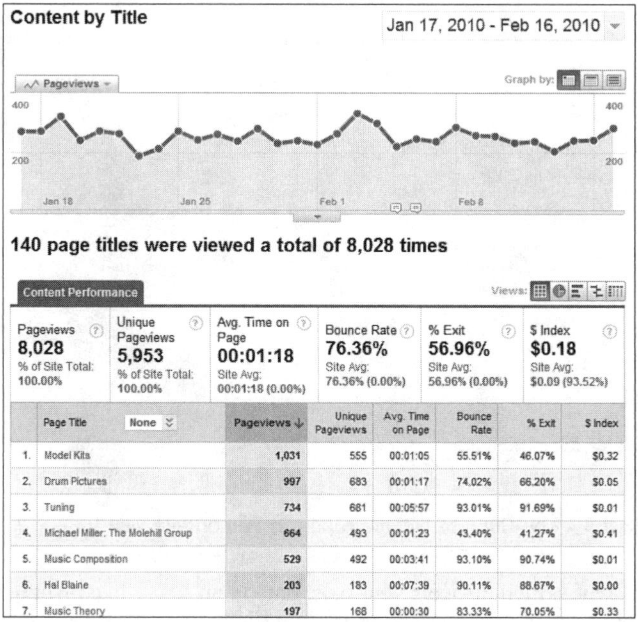

FIGURE 8.7 The Content by Title report in Table view.

You can also display this data in other views, by clicking one of the Views buttons at the top right of the table. The following views are available:

▶ **Table**, the default view, which lists your top pages in tabular format, in descending order.

▶ **Percentage**, shown in Figure 8.8, which displays a pie chart showing your top pages as a percentage of overall site traffic—a great way to see visually which are your best-performing pages.

▶ **Performance**, which lists your top pages in descending order with a bar chart for each page showing its performance using a second metric.

▶ **Comparison**, which also lists your top pages in descending order but displays a bar chart for each page showing how it compares to the average of the chosen metric for your site.

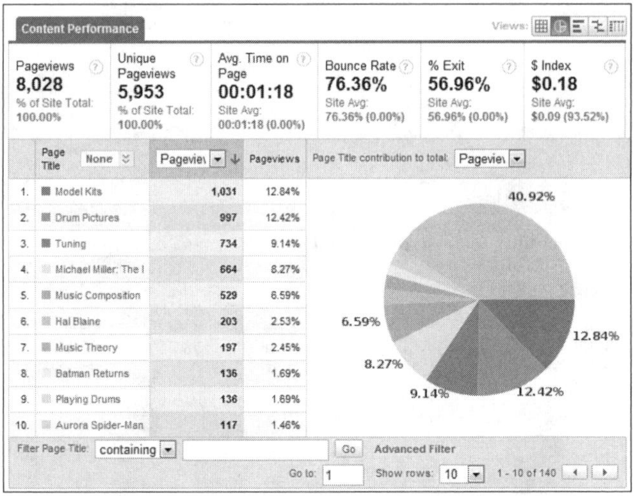

FIGURE 8.8   The Content by Title report in Percentage view.

▶ **Pivot**, which displays your page data in an Excel-like pivot table that correlates each page with your top entrance sources, as shown in Figure 8.9.

Viewing Top Landing Pages

At what pages do people enter your site? It's not necessarily your home page, as other sites and search engines can point to specific pages anywhere in your site structure.

To view a list of these top landing pages, select Content > Top Landing Pages from the left pane of the Dashboard. This displays the Top Landing Pages report, shown in Figure 8.10. As with similar reports, you can display this data in various views; the Percentage view is particularly useful in presenting the top landing pages as a percentage of all entrances on your site.

FIGURE 8.9   Correlating your top page to your top entrance sources.

FIGURE 8.10   The Top Landing Pages report in Percentage view.

Viewing Top Exit Pages

Equally important are the last pages visitors view before leaving your site. This is especially key if you want your visitors to exit from a particular page (a checkout confirmation page, for example), but find them leaving from another page (pre-checkout?) instead.

To view a list of your top exit pages, select Content > Top Exit Pages from the left pane of the Dashboard. The resulting Top Exit Pages report is similar to the Top Landing Pages report, but displaying the last pages visited instead of the first.

Summary

In this lesson, you learned how to analyze the content of your site. In the next lesson, you learn how to track the performance of any AdSense ads you have on your site.

LESSON 9

Tracking AdSense Performance

In this lesson, you learn how to track the performance of AdSense ads on your website.

Understanding Google AdSense

If you want your website to generate revenue, the most common approach is to enable advertising on your site. Since you're (probably) not in the business of selling ad space, you need to partner with an advertising network that brokers space between advertisers and host websites. The ad network will place ads on your site, sell those ads to interested advertisers, and split the advertising revenue with you.

The largest such ad network on the Internet is Google AdSense (www. google.com/adsense). The AdSense network places pay-per-click (PPC) text and image ads on your web pages. You get paid whenever a visitor clicks on one of these ads.

> NOTE: **PPC Advertising**
> With PPC advertising, the advertiser pays the ad network only when customers click on the link in the ad. (The link typically points to the advertiser's website—or, most commonly, a special landing page on the website.) If no one clicks, the advertiser doesn't pay anyone anything. The more clicks that are registered, the more the advertiser pays.

When you sign up for AdSense, you agree to provide Google with access to your website's content. Google needs this access in order to provide ads that are relevant to the content of your site. Google then provides you with a short piece of HTML code to insert in your page's underlying code; this code inserts the PPC ads on a real-time basis.

Whenever someone visits your page, this code reports back to Google. Google then consults its database for information about your page content and serves up one or more PPC ads that match that content. It all happens in real time; the ad appears almost instantaneously with the visitor opening the page.

The PPC ads served by Google AdSense are typically small text or image ads, like the ones shown in Figure 9.1. Multiple small ads are typically grouped into a larger ad unit; you choose where the ad unit is displayed on your web page.

Insurance for Expats	AUTO insurance	GE Healthymagination
International Health Insurance	quotes and protection online auto,	Learn how GE health technology is
Online Quote or Call 1-800-672-	home, renters, condo	reducing the cost of health care
6089	allstateagencies.com/donaldkeller	www.healthymagination.com
www.norfolkmobility.com		

Ads by Google

FIGURE 9.1   A typical block of AdSense text ads.

At the end of each month, Google tallies up how many users have clicked on those ads appearing on your site. It does the internal accounting, based on the amount paid by each advertiser, and then determines your share of the revenues. This money is then deposited electronically into your bank account.

The amount of work you have to do is minimal. There's the sign-up process, of course, which requires you to fill in a few forms and supply your bank account information (so you can get paid). You then have to insert the AdSense code into each page on your site, which is the majority of the work—but a one-time thing. Past that, just sit back and let the process work. (And collect your money at the end of each month, of course.)

How much money can you expect to generate from being a member of Google's AdSense network? It's impossible to tell. It all depends on how much traffic your website generates, the quality of the content you have on your site, and how popular that content is with advertisers. Some website owners generate hundreds and thousands of dollars a month in ad revenue; others generate just a few dollars. Obviously, the bigger and more popular your site, the more potential there is for higher revenues.

> **NOTE: Using Google AdWords and AdSense**
>
> Learn more about Google AdSense in my companion book, *Using Google AdWords and AdSense* (Michael Miller, Que, 2010).

Integrating AdSense with Google Analytics

You can track your AdSense performance from the AdSense website, or you can integrate AdSense with Google Analytics and track your AdSense performance there. In fact, Google Analytics provides more tracking options than AdSense itself does!

You can use Google Analytics to analyze various aspects of your site's traffic—how many people are visiting, which pages they're visiting, how long they stay, where they came from, where they visit next, where they leave the site, and so forth. With this information in hand, you can then fine-tune your site to increase traffic and generate higher AdSense ad revenues.

To link your AdSense account with Google Analytics, follow these steps:

1. Go to the Google AdSense website (www.google.com/adsense/) and sign into your account.

2. From the AdSense Dashboard, shown in Figure 9.2, select the Reports tab, and then the Overview sub-tab.

3. Click the Go to Your Google Analytics Account link.

4. When the next page appears, select I Already Have a Google Analytics Account.

5. Click the Continue button to proceed; then follow the onscreen instructions from there.

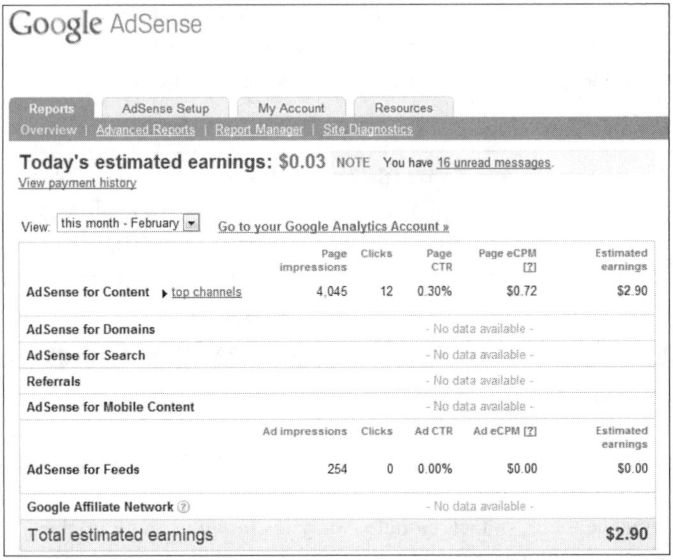

FIGURE 9.2   Linking Google AdSense to your Google Analytics account.

Viewing the AdSense Overview Report

Once linked, information about your AdSense ads now appears in the Google Analytics Dashboard. A variety of reports are available, starting with the AdSense Overview report, shown in Figure 9.3.

To display the AdSense Overview Report, select Content > AdSense > Overview in the left pane of the Dashboard. The overview graph at the top of this page tracks AdSense revenue per day for the past 30 days. As with all overview reports, you can pull down the list at the top-right side of the page to select a different date range, or click the tab at the top-left side of the page to graph a variety of other metrics.

Beneath the overview graph is a list of these other metrics, displaying data for the selected timeframe. These metrics include the following:

> ▶ **AdSense Revenue**, which tracks the revenue generated from your AdSense for Content ads.

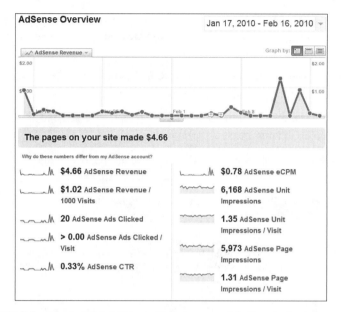

FIGURE 9.3   Viewing the AdSense Overview report in Google Analytics.

▶ **AdSense Revenue/1000 Visits**, which calculates the revenue generated per 1,000 user visits. It's a good way to compare revenue between sites or pages with varying traffic levels.

▶ **AdSense Ads Clicked**, which tracks the total number of clicks on AdSense ads by site visitors.

▶ **AdSense Ads Clicked/Visit**, which tracks the number of clicks on AdSense ads per customer visit. This is a good metric for estimating how your total clicks might increase if you were to increase site traffic.

▶ **AdSense CTR**, which calculates the click-through rate for the ads on your site.

NOTE: **CTR**
Click-through rate (CTR) measures the percentage of people who saw an ad and then clicked that ad. Obviously, a higher CTR is better.

► **AdSense eCPM**, which calculates the effective cost per thousand impressions—essentially, your estimated earnings for every 1,000 impressions.

► **AdSense Unit Impressions**, a useful metric that tracks the number of times ad units are shown on your site.

► **AdSense Unit Impressions/Visit**, which tracks the number of times ad units are shown per customer visit.

► **AdSense Page Impressions**, which tracks the total number of pages viewed by site visitors that include AdSense ads.

► **AdSense Page Impressions/Visit**, which measures the number of pages viewed per customer visit.

Click any of these items to view a more detailed report for that metric. For example, Figure 9.4 shows the AdSense CTR graph and table.

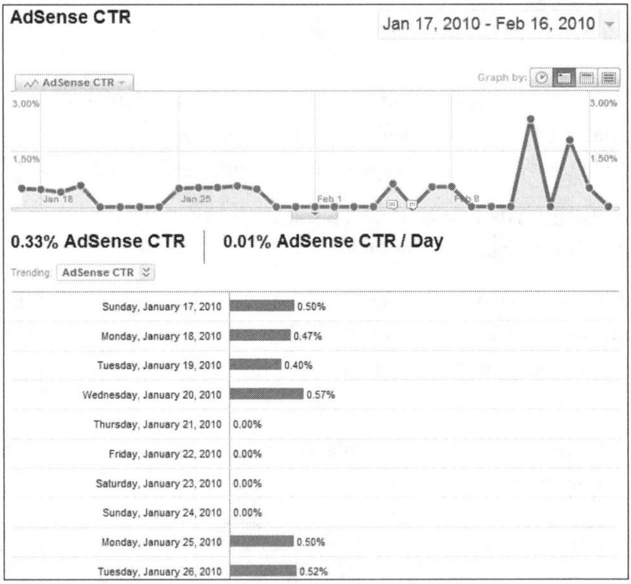

FIGURE 9.4   Viewing the AdSense CTR graph and table.

At the bottom of the AdSense Overview page is the AdSense Details section, which displays two pieces of information. The Top AdSense Content report details revenue from the top-performing pages on your site; the Top AdSense Referrers report tracks revenue by the top traffic sources coming to your site. Click the View Full Report beneath each of these summaries to view the full reports, which we'll discuss next.

Viewing Top AdSense Content

You can place AdSense ads on as many pages on your website as you like. When you have ads on multiple pages, it's good to track the performance of the individual pages. Pages with better or more relevant content typically produce higher click-through rates for the ads that appear on those pages.

To display a list of your top-performing ad pages, select Content > AdSense > Top AdSense Content in the left page of the Google Analytics Dashboard. This displays the Top AdSense Content report, shown in Figure 9.5.

The top of this report is given over to the expected overview graph. Beneath the graph is a list of the top-ten highest ad revenue pages on your site; click the right arrow button beneath the list to display the next ten pages, and the next, and the next.

For each page listed, Google displays the following metrics:

- ▶ AdSense Revenue
- ▶ AdSense Ads Clicked
- ▶ AdSense Page Impressions
- ▶ AdSense CTR
- ▶ AdSense eCPM

To view more detailed information about any individual page, click that page in the table. This displays an AdSense Content report for that individual page.

FIGURE 9.5   Viewing the Top AdSense Content report.

Viewing Top AdSense Referrers

Also of interest are those sites that link to or refer visitors to your site who then click an ad to generate AdSense revenue. These sites are listed in the Top AdSense Referrers report, shown in Figure 9.6. You display this report by selecting Content > AdSense > Top AdSense Referrers.

This report lists the top ten referring sites, in terms of ad revenue ultimately generated. Additional sites can be displayed by clicking the right arrow button underneath the list.

For each site listed, Google displays the same metrics shown in the Top AdSense Content report—AdSense Revenue, AdSense Ads Clicked, AdSense Page Impressions, AdSense CTR, and AdSense eCPM. It's a good way to see which referring sites generate the most revenue for you.

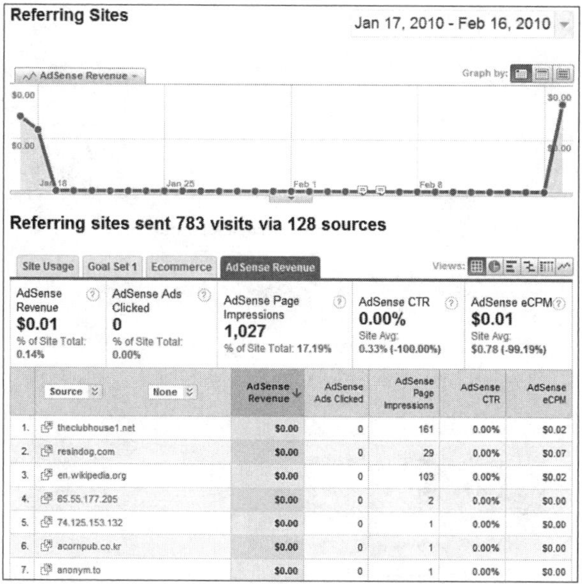
Referring Sites
Jan 17, 2010 - Feb 16, 2010
AdSense Revenue
Graph by:
Referring sites sent 783 visits via 128 sources
Site Usage
Goal Set 1
Ecommerce
AdSense Revenue
Views:
AdSense Revenue $0.01 % of Site Total: 0.14%
AdSense Ads Clicked 0 % of Site Total: 0.00%
AdSense Page Impressions 1,027 % of Site Total: 17.19%
AdSense CTR 0.00% Site Avg: 0.33% (-100.00%)
AdSense eCPM $0.01 Site Avg: $0.78 (-99.19%)
Source
None
AdSense Revenue
AdSense Ads Clicked
AdSense Page Impressions
AdSense CTR
AdSense eCPM
1. theclubhouse1.net $0.00 0 161 0.00% $0.02
2. resindog.com $0.00 0 29 0.00% $0.07
3. en.wikipedia.org $0.00 0 103 0.00% $0.02
4. 65.55.177.205 $0.00 0 2 0.00% $0.00
5. 74.125.153.132 $0.00 0 1 0.00% $0.00
6. acornpub.co.kr $0.00 0 1 0.00% $0.00
7. anonym.to $0.00 0 1 0.00% $0.00

FIGURE 9.6 Viewing the Top AdSense Referrers report.

Viewing AdSense Revenue Trends

If you want to see how your AdSense ads are performing over time, display the AdSense Revenue report, shown in Figure 9.7. You open this report by selecting Content > AdSense > AdSense Trending from the left pane of the Dashboard. This report displays ad revenue per day, which gives you a good indication of whether your ad performance is improving over time. You can also, if you like, display revenue by hour, week, or month, by clicking the appropriate buttons in the Graph By section above overview graph.

FIGURE 9.7   Viewing AdSense performance by day.

Summary

In this lesson, you learned how to track AdSense ad performance in Google Analytics. In the next lesson, you learn how to view Google Analytics Site Overlay report.

LESSON 10

Viewing the Site Overlay Report

In this lesson, you learn how to view link performance on your site with the Site Overlay report.

Understanding the Site Overlay

Most of Google Analytics reports are text-based in nature, sometimes accompanied by a line graph. But there's one report that's much more visual—in fact, it overlays its data on your own web pages.

The Site Overlay report, as the name implies, consists of data overlaid on your web pages. This data details the number of clicks each link on your page receives; you navigate your page as a regular visitor would, and then you discover how popular each page you link to is.

> NOTE: **Clicks/Pageviews**
> The "clicks" metric displayed on the Site Overlay report is based on the number of pageviews received by the linked-to page. This means that if the same page is linked to more than once on a given page, all links will display the same "clicks" (pageviews) number.

Figure 10.1 shows an overlay on a typical web page. With the overlay displayed, each link on the page displays a percentage value. This percentage reflects the percentage of total internal clicks received by a given link. So, for example, if you see a link with 5.1% displayed, that link received 5.1% of all the clicks on internal links received on this page.

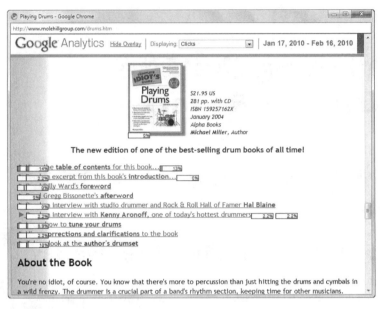

FIGURE 10.1   Part of a web page displayed along with its site overlay; click percentages appear next to each link.

More information is displayed when you hover over a link. This displays an info box, like the one shown in Figure 10.2. This info box contains the link-to URL, the total number of clicks received by this link, and the contribution of this link toward your stated goal.

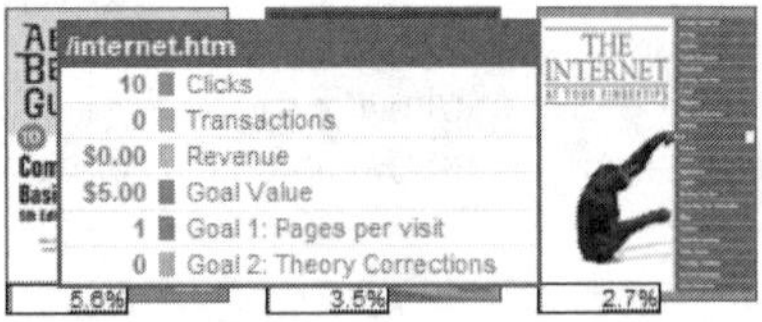

FIGURE 10.2   More information displayed for the selected link.

You can click any link to go to the linked-to page, just as you would on a normal site visit. You then see a new overlay for the next page.

> **NOTE: Limitations**
> The Site Overview report does track the following types of content: JavaScript links, Flash navigation, CSS content, downloadable files, outbound links, frames, and auto redirects.

Displaying the Site Overlay Report

To display the Site Overlay report, select Content > Site Overlay from the left pane of the Google Analytics Dashboard. This opens a new window with your site's home page displayed, along with the overlay information.

To hide the overlay percentages, click the Hide Overlay link at the top of the overlay window, shown in Figure 10.3. To show the percentages again, click the Show Overlay link.

FIGURE 10.3   Hiding the overlay.

By default, the overlay percentages display the click percentage. To display goal value percent instead, pull down the Displaying list and select Goal Value; other goals you've defined are also listed here.

When you're done viewing the Site Overlay report, click the Close link.

Summary

In this lesson, you learned how to display the Site Overlay report. In the next lesson, you learn how to use Google Analytics to track AdWords traffic.

LESSON 11

Tracking AdWords Traffic

In this lesson, you learn how to monitor AdWords performance from your Google Analytics account.

Understanding Google AdWords

If you want to promote your website or business online, Google's AdWords service is the way to go. AdWords lets you create text or image ads and display those ads on Google search results pages and on third-party websites.

You start by creating an ad campaign. For each campaign, you specify the amount of money you're willing to spend (your daily budget) and the duration of the campaign. Then you create multiple ad groups for that campaign; each ad group is centered on one or more keywords that you purchase. Then, within each ad group, you create one or more advertisements to run when those keywords are triggered. These ads are typically small text ads, like the ones in Figure 11.1, although you can also create small image ads.

FIGURE 11.1   A block of AdWords text ads.

The ads you create are linked to specific keywords that you purchase—or, more accurately, bid on. You specify how much you're willing to pay for each keyword, and your ad is displayed when someone searches for that keyword on Google or on third-party sites with content that's relevant to that keyword.

> NOTE: **Google AdSense**
>
> Google AdWords ads are displayed on sites owned by subscribers to Google's AdSense service. Learn more about AdSense in Lesson 9, "Tracking AdSense Performance."

As an advertiser, you pay only when someone clicks your ad—not when the ad is displayed. This is pay-per-click (PPC) advertising, and the price you bid is the cost-per-click (CPC) you pay.

It's important to track not only how often your ad is displayed (impressions), but how often it's clicked—the click-through-rate (CTR). The higher the CTR for your ad, the more effective it is.

> NOTE: **Using Google AdWords and AdSense**
>
> Learn more about Google AdWords in my companion book, *Using Google AdWords and AdSense* (Michael Miller, Que, 2010).

Linking Google AdWords to Google Analytics

Although Google AdWords offers its own tracking facility, you can also track AdWords performance in Google Analytics by linking your AdWords account to your Google Analytics account. If you have established accounts for both services, follow these steps to link the two:

1. Sign into your Google AdWords account at adwords.google.com.

2. Select the Reporting tab and then select Google Analytics.

3. When the next page appears, select I Already Have a Google Analytics Account; then click Continue.

4. When the next page appears, as shown in Figure 11.2, select your Google Analytics account from the pull-down list.

FIGURE 11.2   Linking Google AdWords and Google Analytics accounts.

5. Make sure the Destination URL Auto-Tagging option is selected.

6. Click the Link My Account button.

7. When the confirmation window appears, click Yes, Continue.

Your AdWords data will now appear in Google Analytics.

Tracking AdWords Campaigns

Once linked, you can now track the performance of your AdWords campaigns from the Traffic Sources section of your Google Analytics page. The most important campaign data is found in the AdWords Campaigns report; access this report by selecting Traffic Sources > AdWords > AdWords Campaigns.

As you can see in Figure 11.3, the AdWords Campaigns report tracks each of your active AdWords campaigns and displays the following metrics:

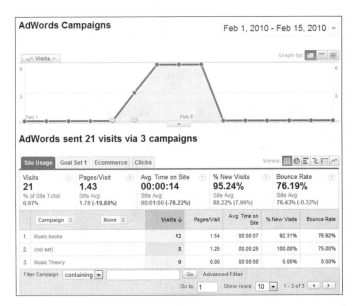

FIGURE 11.3   The main (Site Usage) tab of the AdWords Campaigns report.

▶ **Campaign.** The name of each campaign.

▶ **Visits.** The number of total visits resulting from ad clicks.

▶ **Pages/Visit.** The number of pages seen per visit.

▶ **Avg. Time on Site.** The amount of time each AdWords visitor spent on your site, during an average visit.

▶ **% New Visits.** The percent of AdWords visits from people who had never visited your site before.

▶ **Bounce Rate.** The percent of AdWords visits by visitors who left your site before visiting a second page.

Additional information can be displayed by selecting the Clicks tab below the overview graph. As you can see in Figure 11.4, this displays a wealth of click-related data, including the following:

▶ **Visits.** The number of visits resulting from ad clicks.

FIGURE 11.4   The Clicks tab of the AdWords Campaigns report.

▶ **Impressions.** The number of times your AdWords ads were
   displayed.

▶ **Clicks.** The total number of clicks made on your ads.

▶ **Cost.** The total amount you paid for clicks on your ads.

▶ **CTR.** The percentage of impressions that resulted in clicks.

▶ **CPC.** The average cost you paid for each click on your ad.

▶ **RPC.** The average revenue-per-click you received from each
   click on your ad (if you're selling goods or services on your site).

▶ **ROI.** Return on investment calculated as revenue plus total goal
   value minus your costs, all divided by your costs.

▶ **Margin.** Calculated as revenue plus total goal value minus your
   costs, all divided by revenue.

Tracking Keyword Position

Want to know which of the keywords you purchased are resulting in the
best position on Google's search results pages for your AdWords ads?

Then check out Google Analytics Keyword Positions report, which you display by selecting Traffic Sources > AdWords > Keyword Positions.

By default, this report lists the keywords used in your campaign and the number of visits resulting from each keyword. More useful information is available when you click a keyword, however. This displays a breakdown, like the one shown in Figure 11.5, that shows you how many times this keyword resulted in an ad displayed in the Top 1, Top 2, and Top 3 positions at the top of Google's search results pages. Also shown are the number of times this keyword's ads were displayed in the top positions along the side of Google's search results pages.

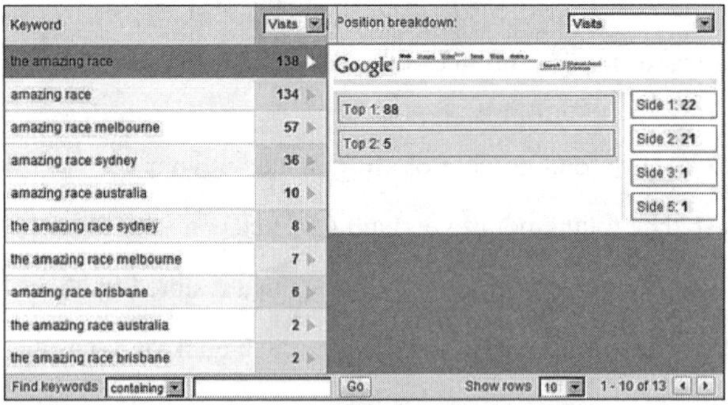

FIGURE 11.5   Displaying the position of ads resulting from the use of a given keyword, in the Keyword Positions report.

NOTE: **Positions**
The top-of-page positions are sometimes referred to as T1, T2, and T3. Side positions are sometimes referred to as S1, S2, S3, and so forth.

Tracking TV Campaigns

It's a little-used feature by most advertisers, but Google offers television advertising through its AdWords program. (Learn more at www.google.com/adwords/tvads/.) If you participate in this program, you can track your television campaigns through Google Analytics.

Select Traffic Sources > AdWords > TV Campaigns to display the TV Campaigns report. The overview graph for this page compares TV impressions with total site visits; the table below the graph displays additional metrics, including TV Plays, Ad Plays, Viewed Entire Ad, % Initial Audience Retained, Cost, and CPM (cost per thousand).

Summary

In this lesson, you learned how to track Google AdWords performance from your Google Analytics account. In the next lesson, you learn how to track the performance of your ecommerce website.

LESSON 12

Tracking Ecommerce

In this lesson, you learn how to use Google Analytics to track ecommerce transactions on your website.

Configuring Google Analytics for Ecommerce Tracking

If you sell goods or services from your website, you can use Google Analytics to track your site's ecommerce performance. Before you do so, however, you have to configure Google Analytics for ecommerce tracking—and configure your shopping cart to report back to Google Analytics.

To configure Google Analytics for ecommerce tracking, follow these steps:

1. From the Google Analytics overview page, click Edit (in the Actions column) for the profile you want to configure.

2. When the Profile Settings page appears, go to the Main Website Profile Information section and click the Edit link.

3. When the Edit Profile Information page appears, as shown in Figure 12.1, scroll to the E-Commerce Website section and check the Yes option.

4. Click the Save Changes button.

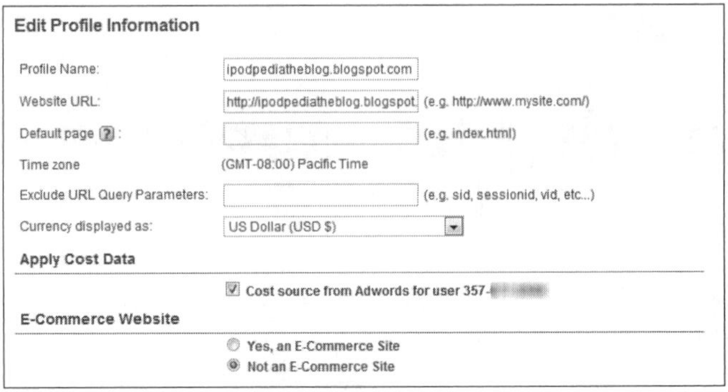

FIGURE 12.1   Configuring Google Analytics for ecommerce tracking.

Configuring Your Receipt Page for Google Analytics Tracking

You now need to configure your website to report sales data to Google Analytics. You do so by inserting the standard Google Analytics tracking code into the source code or your website's sales receipt page (the last page of your checkout process).

Next, you need to establish a transaction, which you do by calling the **_addTrans()** function, somewhere beneath the Google Analytics tracking code. This function takes the following arguments:

- ▶ Order ID (required)
- ▶ Affiliation or store name (optional)
- ▶ Total (required)
- ▶ Tax (optional)
- ▶ Shipping (optional)
- ▶ City (optional)
- ▶ State (optional)
- ▶ Country (optional)

The code for a typical transaction function call should look something like this:

```
<script type="text/javascript">
  var _gaq = _gaq || [];
  _gaq.push(['_setAccount', 'UA-XXXXX-X']);
  _gaq.push(['_trackPageview']);
  _gaq.push(['_addTrans',
    '1234',              // order ID - required
    'My Store',   // affiliation or store name
    '9.95',              // total - required
    '1.50',              // tax
    '2.00',              // shipping
    'Minneapolis',       // city
    'Minnesota',         // state or province
    'USA'                // country
  ]);

  // add item might be called for every item in the shopping
cart
  // where your ecommerce engine loops through each item in
the cart and
  // prints out _addItem for each
  _gaq.push(['_addItem',
    '1234',              // order ID - required
    'DD44',              // SKU/code
    'Mens Shoes',        // product name
    'Brown leather',     // category or variation
    '9.95',              // unit price - required
    '1'                  // quantity - required
  ]);
  _gaq.push(['_trackTrans']); //submits transaction to the
Analytics servers

  (function() {
    var ga = document.createElement('script'); ga.type =
'text/javascript'; ga.async = true;
    ga.src = ('https:' == document.location.protocol ?
'https://ssl' : 'http://www') + '.google-analytics.com/ga.js';
    (document.getElementsByTagName('head')[0] ||
document.getElementsByTagName('body')[0]).appendChild(ga);
  })();
</script>
```

Obviously, you replace all the data examples with your own data; you also replace the UA-XXXXX-X item with your own Google Analytics account number.

Establishing Purchase Items

As you saw in the previous code, you use the **_addItem**() method to detail each item the visitor purchases. This method takes the following arguments:

- ▶ Order ID (required)
- ▶ SKU or Code (optional)
- ▶ Product Name (optional)
- ▶ Category (optional)
- ▶ Price (required)
- ▶ Quantity (required)

This code should be inserted as part of the general ecommerce tracking code, below the Google Analytics tracking code on the receipt page.

Tracking Sales from a Third-Party Shopping Cart

If you use a third-party shopping cart—that is, if your site sends the checkout process to another website—then you need to insert a different piece of JavaScript code.

Inserting the Tracking Code

Begin by inserting a modified version of the Google Analytics tracking code on both your store site and your shopping cart pages, as follows:

```
<script type="text/javascript">
var gaJsHost = (("https:" == document.location.protocol) ?
"https://ssl." : "http://www.");
```

```
document.write(unescape("%3Cscript src='" + gaJsHost + "google-
analytics.com/ga.js' type='text/javascript'%3E%3C/script%3E"));
</script>

<script type="text/javascript">
var pageTracker = _gat._getTracker("UA-xxxxxx-x");
pageTracker._setDomainName("none");
pageTracker._setAllowLinker(true);
pageTracker._trackPageview();
</script>
```

The extra lines are the three that begin with **pageTracker**. Obviously, replace the "UA-xxxxxx-x" with your Google Analytics account number.

Changing Your Links

You now need to change the links from your store site to the secure check-out site. If your current links look something like this:

```
<a href=<a
href="https://www.securecart.com/?store=parameters">Purchase
Now</a>
```

You should change them to the following:

```
<a href=" https://www.securecart.com/?store=parameters"
onclick="pageTracker._link(this.href); return false;">Purchase
Now</a>
```

> NOTE: **Position**
> If your pages include calls to **_trackPageview(), _link(),
> _trackTrans(), or _linkByPost()**, you must insert the Google
> Analytics tracking code before any of these calls. The tracking code
> can be placed anywhere between the opening **<body>** tag and
> these JavaScript calls.

If your shopping cart uses forms, use the following code:

```
<form name="post_form" method="post"
onsubmit="pageTracker._linkByPost(this)">
```

Viewing Ecommerce Reports

Once everything has been configured, you now see an Ecommerce section in the top-left pane of the Google Analytics Dashboard. There are seven primary ecommerce reports available, along with three product performance reports.

Ecommerce Overview

You open the Ecommerce Overview report by selecting Ecommerce > Overview from the top-left pane of the Google Analytics Dashboard. This report, shown in Figure 12.2, opens with an overview graph that displays the ecommerce conversion rate by day for the past month. Beneath this graph are the following metrics:

FIGURE 12.2   The Ecommerce Overview report.

- ▶ **Conversion Rate.** The percentage of visitors who converted to paying customers.

- ▶ **Transactions.** The total number of sales transactions.

- ▶ **Average Order Value.** The average value of an order placed.

▶ **Purchased Products.** How many individual products were purchased.

In addition, the Revenue Analysis section contains links to more in-depth reports. The Visitors Profile reports let you examine the languages and locations of your customers, the Traffic Sources reports tell you which keywords and other sources led to sales, and the Map Overlay shows where your paying customers came from, geographic location-wise.

At the very bottom of this page is the Top Revenue Sources section. These tables display your top-selling products and services.

Total Revenue

When you want to examine your revenue flow by day, select Ecommerce > Total Revenue to display the Total Revenue report. This report provides your revenue totals on a daily basis. (You can also view by hour, week, and month.)

Conversion Rate

What percentage of your visitors converted into paying customers? Select Ecommerce > Conversion Rate to display a graph and list of conversion rates by day for the selected time period.

Average Order Value

To view the average order of values placed on your site, select Ecommerce > Average Order Value to display the Average Order Value report. This report lists the average transaction value by day for the selected time period. (You can also view by hour, week, and month.)

Transactions

Information about individual transactions can be found in the Transactions report, which you access by selecting Ecommerce > Transactions. The top of this report displays revenue by date; the bottom of the report, shown in Figure 12.3, displays the following data for each transaction: Revenue,

Tax, Shipping, and Quantity. Additional data are available by clicking an individual transaction link.

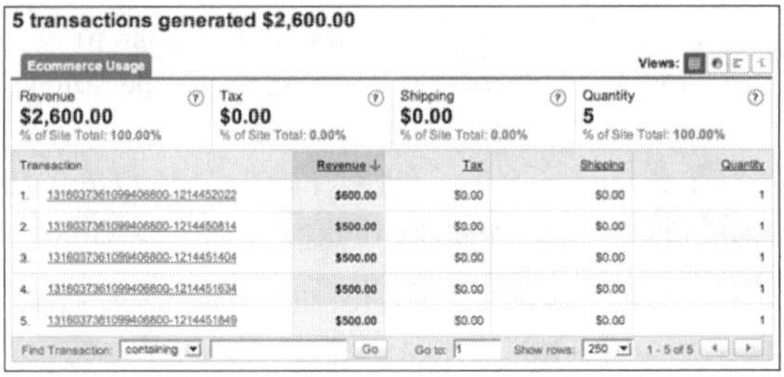

FIGURE 12.3   The Ecommerce Transactions report.

Visits to Purchase

You can gain a better understanding of your site's effectiveness by tracking how many visits it takes a customer to make a single purchase. These data are tracked in the Visits to Purchase report; select Ecommerce > Visits to Purchase. For each number (one visit, two visits, and so on), this report displays the number of transactions involved and the percentage of all purchases this metric represents.

Days to Purchase

Also important is how many days it takes a customer to purchase an item—the total number of days from first visit to purchase. These data are displayed in the Days to Purchase report; select Ecommerce > Days to Purchase. As with the Visits to Purchase report, this report lists the number of transactions and the percentage of all purchases for each possible time-frame.

Product Performance

Google Analytics also offers three reports that look at your site's product performance. These reports include the following:

► **Product Overview** (Ecommerce > Product Performance > Product Overview), which tracks each product sold on your site.

For each product, this report lists Quantity Sold, Unique
Purchases, Product Revenue, Average Price, and Average QTY.
(Figure 12.4 displays the Product Overview report.)

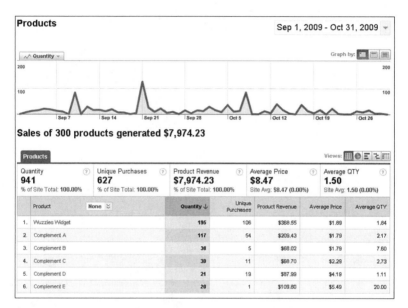

FIGURE 12.4   The Ecommerce Product Overview report.

▶ **Product SKUs** (Ecommerce > Product Performance > Product
SKUs), which displays the same data as the Product Overview
report, but by SKU number instead of product name.

▶ **Categories** (Ecommerce > Product Performance > Categories),
which tracks the same data, but by product category rather than
individual product.

Summary

In this lesson, you learned how to track product sales with Google
Analytics. In the next lesson, you learn how to measure site search usage.

LESSON 13

Measuring Site Search Usage

In this lesson, you learn how to track your visitor's use of search on your site.

Understanding Site Search

If you have a fairly large website, you can make it easier for your visitors to find specific content by including some sort of mechanism to search your site. More often than not, this takes the form of a Google-like search box and accompanying search button, like the ones in Figure 13.1; visitors type their queries into the search box, click the Search button, and then see a list of pages on your site that match their queries.

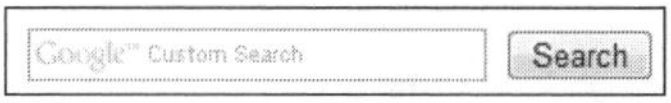

FIGURE 13.1 A typical search box (this one's from Google) for searching an individual website.

What your site visitors are searching for can tell you a lot about them—and about your site. You can learn what terms are most searched for, which pages come up most often in search results, and the paths that visitors take after they've completed their searches.

All of this information is available from Google Analytics, once you've configured Analytics for your site's search engine.

> NOTE: **Google Site Search Options**
> One of the most popular website search engines is Google Site Search (www.google/com/sitesearch/), available for as little as

$100/year. Google also offers the free Custom Search Engine (www.google.com/cse/), which you can easily embed in your site's HTML code. And if you have a Blogger blog, you can add Google blog search via a simple sidebar widget.

Configuring Google Analytics to Track Site Search

Before Google Analytics can track your internal site search data, you must configure Analytics for your specific search engine. Follow these steps:

1. From the Google Analytics Overview page, click the Edit link for the account you want to track.

2. On the Profile Settings page, click the Edit link in the Main Website Profile Information section.

3. On the Edit Profile Information page, scroll to the Site Search section, shown in Figure 13.2, and select the Do Track Site Search option. This expands the page to show additional site search options.

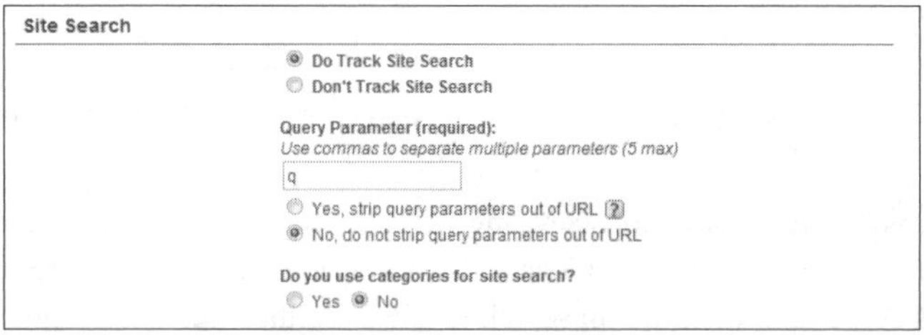

Site Search

⦿ Do Track Site Search
○ Don't Track Site Search

Query Parameter (required):
Use commas to separate multiple parameters (5 max)

q

○ Yes, strip query parameters out of URL ?
⦿ No, do not strip query parameters out of URL

Do you use categories for site search?
○ Yes ⦿ No

FIGURE 13.2   Configuring Google Analytics to track internal site search data.

4. In the Query Parameter box, enter the word or words that your search engine uses to designate an internal query. Different search engines use different parameters, but most often this is the single letter "q." (Sometimes it's the single letter "s.")

5. If your site uses unique session IDs or other query parameters in its URLs, you can exclude these parameters by checking Yes, Strip Query Parameters Out of URL.

6. If you use categories for site search, check the Yes option and enter those categories into the Category Parameter box; separate multiple categories with commas. Otherwise, check the No option.

7. Click the Save Changes button.

> NOTE: **Search Parameters**
>
> If you're not sure what query parameter your site search engine uses, or if you search by category, consult your search engine's help facility for more information.

Viewing Site Search Reports

Once you have Google Analytics properly configured for site search, you now see a variety of Site Search reports in the Content section of the left pane of the Google Analytics Dashboard. These reports let you see how people search your site—what they search for, where they begin their searches, which pages they visit as a result of their searches, and so forth.

Site Search Overview

The most immediately useful report is the Site Search Overview, shown in Figure 13.3. You display this report by selecting Content > Site Search > Overview from the left pane of the Google Analytics Dashboard.

The overview graph at the top of the page tracks how many visits utilized site search on a daily basis for the past month. Beneath the graph is a table full of key metrics, including the following:

▶ **Visits with Search**, which tracks the total number of visits that included a site search.

▶ **Total Unique Searches**, which tracks the total number of searches made for the selected time period, excluding multiple searches

FIGURE 13.3   The Site Search Overview report.

on the same keyword during a single visit. (Remember, a single visit can include multiple searches.)

▶ **Results Pageviews/Search**, which tracks how many pageviews resulted from site searches.

▶ **Search Exits**, which tracks the number of searches made immediately before leaving your site, divided by the total number of visits with search.

▶ **Search Refinements**, which tracks the number of times visitors searched again immediately after performing their searches.

▶ **Time After Search**, which tracks the average amount of time visitors spend on your site after performing a search.

▶ **Search Depth**, which tracks the average number of pages visitors viewed after performing a search.

Additional reports are available by clicking the links to the right of the key metrics. In addition, the Site Search Details section at the bottom of the page displays your Top Site Searches and Top Searched Content; click the View Full Report links to view longer lists for these metrics.

Usage

You use the Site Search Usage report to learn if visitors are using your site search function. If you discover that few visitors are searching your site, for example, you might choose to remove the search function.

To view the Site Search Usage report, select Content > Site Search > Usage from the left pane of the Dashboard. The main section of this report, shown in Figure 13.4, displays data for visits both with and without site search, along with a pie chart graphically displaying this data.

FIGURE 13.4   The Site Search Usage report.

Search Terms

To learn more about what keywords and key phrases visitors are searching for, display the Search Terms report, shown in Figure 13.5. You display this report by selecting Content > Site Search > Search Terms from the left pane of the Dashboard.

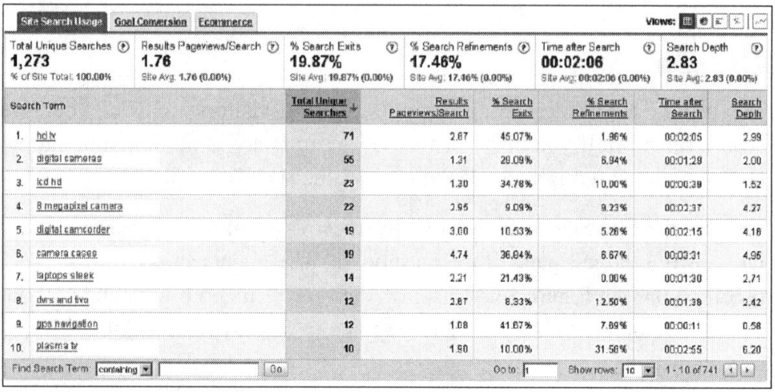

FIGURE 13.5   The Search Terms report.

This report lists the top search queries, with the following data for each query:

▶ **Search Term.** The keyword or key phrase that visitors searched for.

▶ **Total Unique Searches.** The total searches made for the particular search term.

▶ **Results Pageviews/Search.** The number of pageviews resulting from the selected search.

▶ **% Search Exits.** The percentage of visitors who left your site immediately after concluding a search for this term.

▶ **% Search Refinements.** The percentage of visitors who conducted another search after searching for this term.

▶ **Time After Search.** The average amount of time visitors spent on your site after searching for this term.

► **Search Depth.** The average number of pages viewed after visitors searched for this term.

Start Pages

What pages were people viewing when they decided to search your site? That information is available in the Start Pages report. Access this report by selecting Content > Site Search > Start Pages from the left pane of the Dashboard. This report identifies the top pages visitors were on when they initiated their searches and the number of searches initiated from each page.

Destination Pages

Similarly, the Destination Pages report lists those pages that visitors went to after completing their searches and the number of searches that led to each page. Access this report by selecting Content > Site Search > Destination Pages from the left pane of the Dashboard.

> NOTE: **Keyword Searches**
> Click a page listed in the Destination Pages report to display which keyword searches led to the page.

Categories

If you allow category searching within your site, you can view which categories were most searched by displaying the Site Search Categories report. Display this report by selecting Content > Site Search > Categories from the left pane of the Dashboard.

Trending

You can view site search statistics over time by displaying the Site Search Trending report (Content > Site Search > Trending). This report tracks the number of visits with site search by day, week, month, or hour. You can also track trends for other metrics (Total Unique Searches, Results

Pageviews/Search, % Search Exits, % Search Refinements, Time After Search, and Search Depth) by making new selections from the Trending pull-down list.

Summary

In this lesson, you learned how to track usage of your website's internal site search function. In the next lesson, you learn how to configure Google Analytics to track goals and funnels.

LESSON 14

Setting Up Goals and Funnels

In this lesson, you learn how to define and set up goals and funnels in your Google Analytics account.

Understanding Goals and Funnels

In many instances, you want visitors to your website to perform a specified action. Perhaps you want your visitors to make a purchase, fill in a form, or just view a particular page.

In Google Analytics, a goal is defined as a visit to a particular page. As such, you have to translate your internal goals into visits to specific goal pages. When a visitor visits that goal page, you get a *conversion*—that is, your goal is accomplished.

For a purchase, for example, that goal page may be the purchase confirmation page. For a form, the goal page may be a thank-you page after the person has submitted the form. The goal page also can be any specific page on your site to which you want to drive visitors.

The path that you expect visitors to take on their way to reaching the goal page is called a *funnel*. By examining the paths that visitors take, you can see how frequently visitors both achieve and abandon your stated goals, and where they go when they vary from the path.

For example, a funnel on an ecommerce site might include the first page of the checkout process, the shipping address information page, and finally the credit card information page. If visitors abandon the goal, you need to know where on this path they go astray.

For Google Analytics to track goal conversion metrics, you must first define one or more goals. Specifically, you should give the goal a name, assign an optional dollar value to the goal, and then (optionally) define up to ten pages in a funnel path. Google Analytics can then track how often your goals were achieved.

Defining Your Goals

Google Analytics lets you define three types of goals. As previously discussed, a goal can be a specific page; this is called a *URL destination* goal. A goal can also be a specific amount of *time on site* for each visitor, or a specific number of *pages per visit*. These last two goals are more about keeping the visitor on the site rather than performing a specific activity.

To define a goal within Google Analytics, follow these steps:

1. From the Google Analytics Overview page, click the Edit link for the account for which you want to set a goal.

2. When the Profile Settings page appears, scroll to the Goals section, shown in Figure 14.1, and click the Add Goal link for Goals (Set 1).

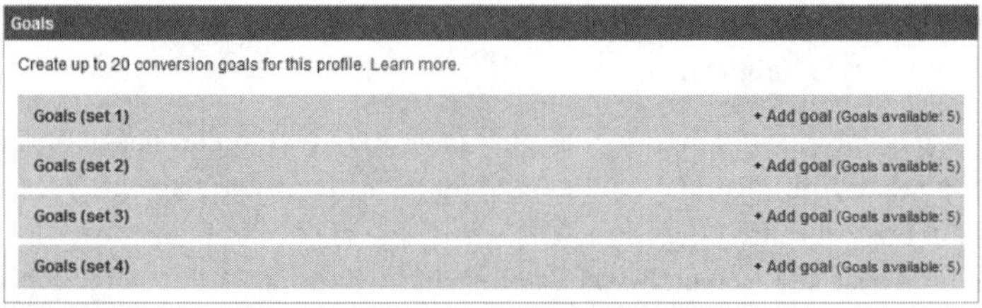

FIGURE 14.1   Adding goals to a website profile.

3. When the Goal Settings page appears, as shown in Figure 14.2, enter a name for this goal into the Goal Name box.

4. To activate this goal, select the Active Goal On option.

5. Pull down the Goal Position list and select the position for this goal. If this is your first goal, select Set 1, Goal 1.

6. In the Goal Type section, select the type of goal: URL Destination, Time on Site, or Pages/Visit.

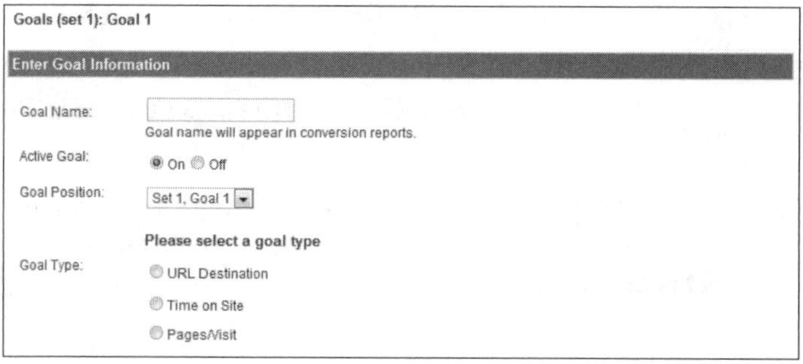

FIGURE 14.2 Defining a new goal.

7. The bottom section of this page now expands, depending on the selection you made in Step 6. If you selected URL Destination, select the Match Type, Goal URL, whether the URL is Case Sensitive, and the Goal Value. If you selected Time on Site, enter the desired time (in hours, minutes, and seconds), and then enter a Goal Value. If you selected Pages/Visit, enter the target number of pages, along with a Goal Value.

> NOTE: **Match Types**
>
> There are three ways to match a URL Destination goal. These match types include *head match* (used for matching dynamic web pages), *exact match* (used for matching full regular URLs), and *regular expression match* (used for matching partial URLs).

8. Click the Save Goal button.

If you want to enter additional goals, repeat these steps.

> NOTE: **Goals**
>
> You can define up to four sets of goals, each containing five individual goals, for 20 goals total per website profile.

Defining Funnels

If you created a URL Destination goal, you can then define a funnel for this goal—the path you desire visitors to take through your site to get to the goal page. Start by selecting URL Destination on the Goal Settings page, and then follow these steps:

1. From the Goal Settings page, click Yes, Create a Funnel for This Goal.

2. This expands the Goal Funnel section of the page, as shown in Figure 14.3. Enter the URL and the name of the first page in the funnel path into the Step 1 boxes.

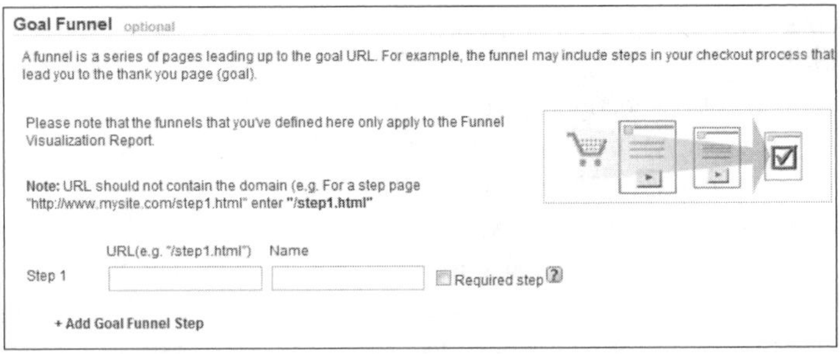

Goal Funnel optional

A funnel is a series of pages leading up to the goal URL. For example, the funnel may include steps in your checkout process that lead you to the thank you page (goal).

Please note that the funnels that you've defined here only apply to the Funnel Visualization Report.

Note: URL should not contain the domain (e.g. For a step page "http://www.mysite.com/step1.html" enter "/step1.html"

URL(e.g. "/step1.html")   Name

Step 1 [   ] [   ] ☐ Required step ⑦

+ Add Goal Funnel Step

FIGURE 14.3   Defining a funnel path.

3. To add a second page to the funnel path, enter the URL and the name of the next page into the Step 2 boxes. Include only the path of the page, not the complete domain URL.

4. Continue to add URLs into the Step boxes to complete the funnel path.

5. Click the Save Goal button when done.

Measuring Your Goals

Once you've defined your goals (and, for URL destination goals, your funnel paths), you can now measure the progress toward your goals—that is, track the number of visits where visitors did what you wanted them to do. You do this via the Goals section on the left pane of the Google Analytics Dashboard.

Overview

As you can see in Figure 14.4, the Goals Overview report (Goals > Overview) is a simple one. This report tracks the total number of conversions for each goal you set—that is, the number of times visitors accomplished the set goals. Beneath this data is the Goal Performance section, which displays your Goal Conversion Rate (what percentage of visits accomplished this goal) and the Total Goal Value (the total dollar value of the accomplished goals, as determined when you first set up the goals).

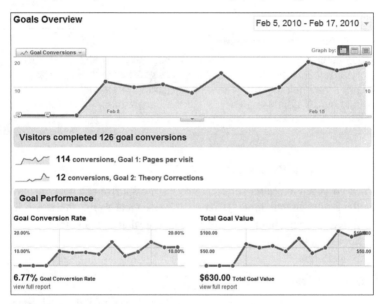

FIGURE 14.4   The Goals Overview report.

Total Conversions

When you want to track conversions over time, open the Total Conversions report (Goals > Total Conversions). This report lists total conversion by hour, day, week, or month for each goal you've defined.

Conversion Rate

The *conversion rate* is the percentage of visits that result in visitors taking the course of action you defined as a goal. The Conversion Rate report

(Goals > Conversion Rate) tracks conversion rate by hour, day, week, or month for each goal you've defined.

Goal Verification

If you have multiple pages that count toward the same goal, you can track the performance of each page separately with the Goal Verification report (Goals > Goal Verification). This report displays each goal page separately and as a percentage of the overall goal.

> NOTE: **Multiple Goal Pages**
> You can create one goal with multiple pages by pointing to a directory or folder rather than an individual page when you set the goal. Rather than pointing to /folder1/page1.htm, for example, you would simply point to /folder1/. All the pages, then, within this folder would count toward a goal conversion.

Reverse Goal Path

When you want to see the different ways visitors arrive at a goal, display the Reverse Goal Path report (Goals > Reverse Goal Path). This report lists the different navigation paths to the selected goal and the number of conversions represented by each path.

Goal Value

If you assigned a dollar value to your goals, you can track the total value of successful conversions via the Goal Value report (Goals > Goal Value). This report displays the monetary value of your goal conversions by hour, day, week, or month.

Goal Abandoned Funnels

If you set up a funnel for a URL destination goal, you want to know how often visitors abandoned the desired path to the goal. To that end, the Goal Abandoned Funnels report (Goals > Goal Abandoned Funnels) displays the abandonment rate (the percentage of visitors who started down the funnel but then left it) by hour, day, week, and month.

Funnel Visualization

It's also informative to see how exactly visitors deviated from the desired navigation path; at what point do they abandon the funnel? This information is presented in the Funnel Visualization report (Goals > Funnel Visualization).

If you're tracking a URL destination goal, this report displays a graphic visualization of each of the steps in your specified funnel path, as shown in Figure 14.5. At each step in the path, you see how many visitors displayed this page, how many moved onto the next page in the path, how many abandoned the path at that point, and the percentage of users who abandoned the path at each point. It's a great, highly visual way to see how successful your goal was—and where in the path your funnel was most often abandoned.

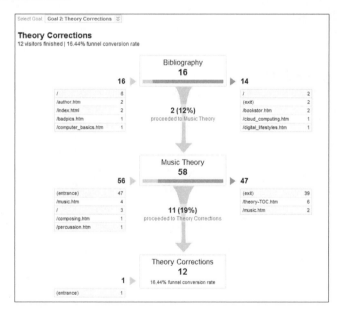

FIGURE 14.5   The Funnel Visualization report.

Summary

In this lesson, you learned how to set up and track goals and funnels. In the next lesson, you learn how to use event tracking.

LESSON 15

Using Event Tracking

In this lesson, you learn how to implement event tracking on your website.

Understanding Event Tracking

When you want to record user interaction with specific elements on your web pages—elements not otherwise tracked by Google Analytics default reports—you need to implement Google Analytics event tracking. Event tracking lets you monitor specific user actions, from clicking "play" on an embedded video to selecting a specific item in a Flash-based menu system. It's all about tracking actions that visitors take with specific elements on your site, rather than just looking at pageviews and clicks.

Defining Events

You can use event tracking to track any or all of the following:

- Flash-driven elements, including menus and video players
- Gadgets and widgets
- File downloads
- Embedded AJAX page elements
- Data load times

Defining Parameters

When you implement event tracking in Google Analytics, you create a piece of script called a *method*, which is then associated with each event you want to track. This piece of code is inserted into the source code for the object you're tracking.

This special method code lets you define four key parameters, which you use to track the event behavior, as follows:

- ▶ **Category.** You use categories to group objects you want to track. This is a required parameter in the event-tracking script.

- ▶ **Action.** This parameter names the type of event or interaction you want to track for a particular web object. This is also a required parameter.

- ▶ **Label.** This parameter provides additional information for events you want to track. This is an optional parameter.

- ▶ **Value.** This parameter is used to assign a numeric value to a tracked object. This is also an optional parameter; unlike the previous parameters, it is a numerical value (integer) rather than a text field (string).

Setting Up Event Tracking

For event tracking to work, you must first have the basic Google Analytics tracking code installed on the page that contains the object you're tracking. (You learned how to do this in Lesson 3, "Adding Google Analytics to Your Website.")

Once you've installed the basic tracking code, you need to construct a **_trackEvent()** method that defines the event you want to track, and then insert that code into the source code for the gadget or web object you want to track. The **_trackEvent()** code takes the following form:

```
pageTracker._trackEvent(category, action, optional_label,
optional_value);
```

As an example, the following piece of code tracks any instance of a user pressing the "play" button (action: "Play") for a video (category: "Videos") titled "Our Vacation" (label: "Our Vacation"):

```
pageTracker._trackEvent('Videos', 'Play', 'Our Vacation');
```

As you can see, the **_trackEvent()** parameters are listed in a specific order (category, action, and label), with each value surrounded by single quotes.

> NOTE: **Multiple Events**
>
> You can include multiple **_trackEvent()** methods to define multiple events for a given item. For example, if you want to track users clicking "play," "stop," and "pause" in a video player, you would create one line of code for each action.

How you call this code depends on the type of object you're tracking. For example, if this event is associated with a video player object, you'd call the code as part of the player's **onClick** action for the "play" command, like this:

```
<a href="#" onClick="pageTracker._trackEvent('Videos', 'Play',
'Our Vacation');">Play</a>
```

For specific instructions on how to install event-tracking code with different types of events and objects, see the help files on the Google Analytics site.

Monitoring Event Tracking

Once you've inserted all the proper codes, you can track the events you've defined via the Event Tracking section of Google Analytics Content reports. You access the event-tracking reports by selecting Content > Event Tracking in the left pane of the Google Analytics Dashboard.

There is an overview report, of course, as well as reports for the three key parameters (categories, actions, and labels). Trending and hostname reports are also available.

Overview

The Event Tracking Overview report (Content > Event Tracking > Overview) tracks the total usage of all the events you've defined. At the top of the page, shown in Figure 15.1, the overview graph tracks total events by day for the past month. Beneath the overview graph are several key metrics, as follows:

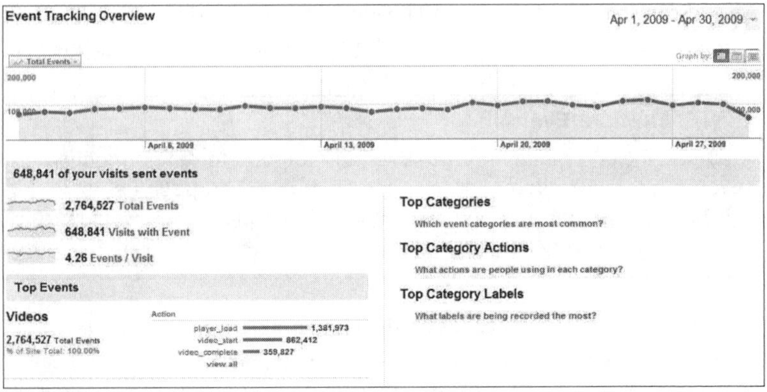

FIGURE 15.1   The Event Tracking Overview report.

▶ **Total Events**, which tracks all the events you've defined.

▶ **Visits with Event**, which tracks the number of customer visits that triggered your defined events.

▶ **Events/Visit**, which calculates the average number of events per visit, by day or hour of day.

Beneath this is a list of your top events, along with links to further reports.

Categories

To track your events by category, open the Event Tracking Categories report (Content > Event Tracking > Categories). This report lists the top categories you've defined for your events; for each category, columns detail the following metrics:

▶ Total Events

▶ Unique Events

▶ Event Value

▶ Average Value

Actions

The Event Tracking Actions report (Content > Event Tracking > Actions) is similar to the Categories report, except it tracks the actions you defined for your events. All actions you've defined are listed here, with the same metrics tracked as in the Categories report.

Labels

Also similar is the Event Tracking Labels report (Content > Event Tracking > Labels), which tracks the labels you defined for your events. Each label is listed, along with the key metrics tracked in the two previous reports.

Trending

The Event Tracking Trending report (Content > Event Tracking > Trending) is used to track events over a defined period. It displays Total Events, Events with Visit, and Events/Visit data per hour, day, week, or month.

Hostnames

The Event Tracking Hostnames report tracks event usage by the hosts used by your site's visitors. The top hostnames are listed, along with Total Events, Event Value, and Average Value for each.

Summary

In this lesson, you learned how to use Google Analytics event-tracking feature. In the next lesson, you learn how to create custom reports in Google Analytics.

LESSON 16

Creating Custom Reports

In this lesson, you learn how to create custom Google Analytics reports.

Understanding Metrics and Dimensions

If the stock reporting isn't to your liking, Google Analytics also lets you create all manner of custom reports. These reports are built around combinations of *metrics* and *dimensions*. We'll look at these components separately.

Metrics

The metrics available in custom reports track important data points. Think of a metric as a column in your report—the more metrics you track, the more columns you add to the report.

There are five types of top-level metrics available, as follows:

- ▶ **Site Usage**, including bounces, bounce rate, entrances, exits, % exit, visitors, new visits, unique visitors, % new visits, time on page, average time on page, pageviews, pages/visit, time on site, average time on site, and visits.

- ▶ **Content**, including unique pageviews, total unique searches, visits with search, search refinements, time after search, search depth, search exits, unique events, event value, and total events.

► **Goals**, including total goal starts, goal1 starts, goal2 starts, goal3 starts, goal4 starts, total goal completions, goal1 completions, goal2 completions, goal3 completions, goal4 completions, total goal value, goal1 value, goal2 value, goal3 value, goal4 value, per visit goal value, goal1 conversion rate, goal2 conversion rate, goal3 conversion rate, goal4 conversion rate, goal conversion rate, goal1 abandonment rate, goal2 abandonment rate, goal3 abandonment rate, goal4 abandonment rate, and total abandonment rate.

► **Ecommerce**, including unique purchases, product revenue, quantity, revenue, per visit value, RPC (revenue per click), average value, shipping, tax, and transactions.

► **Advertising**, including clicks, cost, impressions, CTR (click-through rate), CPC (cost per click), CPM (cost per thousand), cost per goal conversion, cost per transaction, and cost per conversion.

You should be familiar with most of these metrics from their use in Google Analytics standard reports. You can include up to ten metrics (columns) for each tab in your report.

You can build a report using only metrics. In this type of report, there are no restrictions as to which metrics you use.

You can also build a report by crossing metrics against dimensions. In this type of report, the metrics are subject to the limitations defined by the dimensions used.

Dimensions

In a custom report, a dimension is a data field. If a metric is a column in a report, a dimension is a row. You then look at the metrics as they pertain to the selected data

For example, you might choose Visitor Type as your main dimension so that you can look at different types of visitors, such as new and returning. You can then add metrics (columns) to view visitor type by New Visits,

Time on Page, and Pageviews. (This particular report is shown in Figure 16.1.)

FIGURE 16.1   A custom report that tracks Visitor Type (dimension) by New Visits, Time on Page, and Pageviews (metrics).

Google Analytics offers five top-level dimensions, with a number of sub-dimensions, as follows:

▶ **Visitors**, reported by hour of the day, day, week, month, page depth, days since last visit, count of visits, visitor type, city, language, region, country/territory, continent, sub-continent region, and various user-defined values.

▶ **Traffic Sources**, reported by campaign, ad group, keyword, ad content, ad slot, ad slot position, source, medium, source/medium, and referral path.

▶ **Content**, reported by page title, page, site search status, search term, refined keyword, site search category, landing page, exit page, event category, event action, and event label.

▶ **Ecommerce**, reported by affiliation, days to transaction, transaction, product SKU, product, product category, and count of visits to a transaction.

▶ **Systems**, reported by browser, browser version, connection speed, operating system, operating system version, Flash version, Java support, screen colors, screen resolution, hostname, service provider, and domain.

You can select up to five dimensions in a custom report. The first dimension is your top-level table segment; the other four dimensions can be drilled down to in the report.

You can also create reports without dimensions. These reports track only metrics.

Creating a Custom Report

You build a report from a combination of metrics and, if you want, dimensions. Follow these steps:

1. From the Google Analytics Dashboard, click Custom Reporting > Manage Custom Reports from the left pane.

2. When the Manage Custom Reports page appears, click Create New Custom Report.

3. A blank custom report page now appears, as shown in Figure 16.2. To add a metric to the graph, click the data type in the Metrics box in the left pane to expand that type of metric; then drag the individual metric onto one of the metric boxes underneath the graph. Each metric you select adds a new column to your report.

4. Repeat Step 3 to insert additional metrics (columns) into your report.

5. To re-order the columns in your report, use your mouse to drag the metric boxes into a new order.

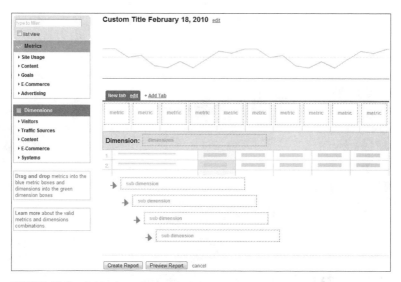

FIGURE 16.2   A blank custom report page.

6. To add a dimension to your report, click the data type in the Dimensions box; then drag a specific item to the Dimension box underneath the graph. The page should now look something like Figure 16.3.

> **NOTE: Dimensions**
>
> Not all dimensions are available for all metrics. Available dimensions for the metrics you've selected are in full-color boxes; dimensions that you can't use are shaded black.

7. To drill down to another level of data, click the data type in the Dimensions box; then drag a specific item to the Sub Dimension box underneath the graph.

8. A report can track additional metrics and dimensions through the use of multiple tabs. To add a new tab to your report, click the Add Tab link; then repeat Steps 3–7 for this new tab.

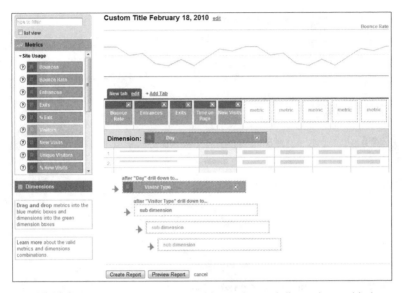

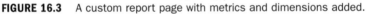

FIGURE 16.3   A custom report page with metrics and dimensions added.

9. Click the Edit link next to the report's title, enter a new title for the report, and then click the Apply button.

10. Click the Preview Report button to see a preview of the report.

11. When your report is completed, click the Create Report button to view the finished report.

Google now generates the report you created and adds the report to the Custom Reporting section of the Dashboard, as well as to the Manage Custom Reports page.

Viewing Your Report

Creating a custom report isn't the last step. There are many ways to customize the view of a custom report, as you'll soon discover.

Changing the Overview Graph

The top of the custom report hosts the overview graph. This graph typically displays the first metric (column) you selected, displaying the data by day for the past month. You can display other metrics by clicking the down arrow on the tab above the report. You can also graph this data by month or week by selecting the appropriate button in the Graph By section above the graph. Finally, you can graph a different timeframe by clicking the down arrow next to the date range above the graph.

Sorting by Metric

Below the graph is the data table. You can sort the data in this table by any column (metric), simply by clicking the metric label at the top of a column.

Selecting Different Views

You can also view your selected data in different ways; you're not limited to the default table view. Most reports have five different views available, as follows:

- ▶ Table (data in row-and-column format)

- ▶ Percentage (data as percentages in a pie chart)

- ▶ Performance (data represented as a bar chart)

- ▶ Comparison (data as comparative percentages in a bar chart)

- ▶ Pivot (data in an interactive pivot table)

Select a different view by clicking the appropriate button in the Views section above the data table.

Visualizing Your Data—in Motion

Finally, Google Analytics offers a unique way to visualize your data, in the form of a motion chart. You display this motion chart by clicking the Visualize button above the overview graph.

As you can see in Figure 16.4, the motion chart graphs each of your dimensions via a series of colored circles. You can opt to vary the size of the circles to represent the comparative amounts for each data point.

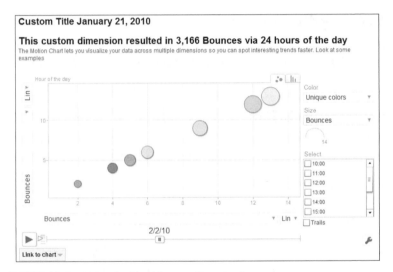

FIGURE 16.4   Data displayed in a motion chart.

The motion in the motion chart comes from adjusting the slider beneath the graph. The graph displays only one day at a time; move the slider to graph other days.

NOTE: **Bars**
To display data points as bars instead of circles, select the bar chart tab above the motion chart.

Revisiting Custom Reports

All custom reports you create are saved in the Custom Reporting panel on the left side of the Dashboard, as shown in Figure 16.5, as well as on the Manage Custom Reports page. To view one of these custom reports, simply click its title in the Custom Reporting panel.

Manage Custom Reports			+ Create new custom report
Design a one of a kind report to fit your needs. Learn how to build a custom report.			
Custom Reports in www.molehillgroup.com			
Name	Dimensions		Action
Custom Title January 21, 2010	Hour of the day	HIDE FROM PROFILE	Edit | Share | Delete
Visitor Types February 9 2010	Visitor Type	HIDE FROM PROFILE	Edit | Share | Delete
Custom Report February 18, 2010	Day , Visitor Type	HIDE FROM PROFILE	Edit | Share | Delete
Search: [ ] Go			1 - 3 of 3 ◀ ▶

FIGURE 16.5   Custom reports displayed in the Custom Reporting panel.

Summary

In this lesson, you learned how to create a custom Google Analytics report. In the next lesson, you learn how to filter the data you see in Google Analytics.

LESSON 17

Filtering Data

In this lesson, you learn how to filter Google Analytics data.

Understanding Filters

You don't always want to track all the traffic coming to your website. You may want to not track internal traffic, for example, or visitors coming from a particular site to yours.

For that matter, you may not want to track all the pages on your site. Perhaps some pages are more important to you than others; maybe you simply want to exclude traffic going to a particular directory or subdomain.

In these instances, you want to filter the data tracked by Google Analytics. You do this by creating a *filter* that automatically excludes data based on your specific parameters.

Google Analytics provides three predefined filter types, as well as the ability to create your own custom filters.

> NOTE: **Order**
> By default, filters are applied in the order in which they were added.

Creating a Predefined Filter

Google Analytics predefined filters are the easiest way to exclude certain types of visitors from appearing in your data and reports. There are three predefined filters that perform the following actions:

► **Exclude all traffic from a domain.** Use this filter to not track visitors who come from a specific website or domain, such as a particular ISP or company network.

► **Exclude all traffic from an IP address.** Use this filter to not track visitors from specific computers or domains. (This filter is used to exclude data from internal traffic sources; learn more in Lesson 20, "Filtering Out Internal Traffic.")

► **Include only traffic to a subdirectory.** Use this filter to report only on traffic to a specific subdirectory on your site.

To create a predefined filter, follow these steps:

1. From the Google Analytics Overview page, click the Filter Manager link (beneath the list of website profiles).

2. When the Filter Manager page appears, click the Add Filter link.

3. When the Create New Filter page appears, as shown in Figure 17.1, enter a name for this filter into the Filter Name box.

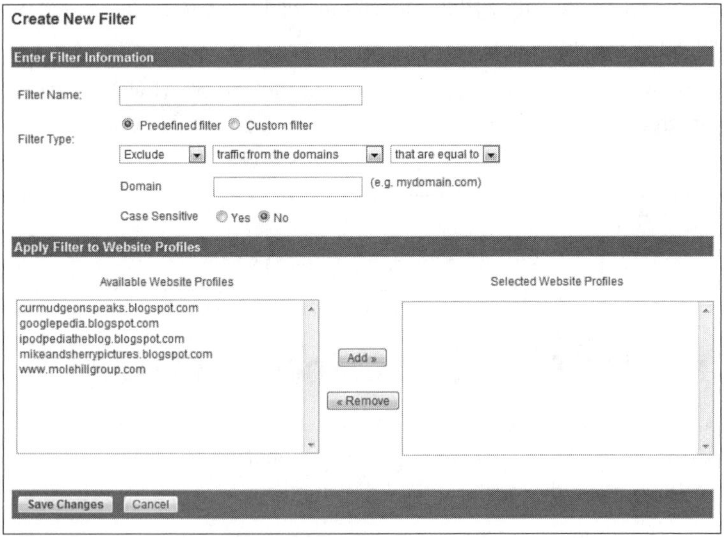

FIGURE 17.1   Creating a new predefined filter.

4. Select the Predefined Filter option.

5. Pull down the first Filter Type list and select whether you want to Exclude traffic or Include Only traffic of a specified type.

6. Pull down the second Filter Type list and select one of the three predefined filters: Traffic from the Domains, Traffic from the IP Addresses, or Traffic to the Subdirectories.

7. Pull down the third Filter Type list and select one of the available options: That are Equal To, That Begin With, That End With, or That Contain.

8. Enter the domain, IP address, or subdirectory that you want to filter into the next box. (This box changes dynamically based on the selection you make in Step 6.)

9. Go to the Apply Filter to Website Profiles section and select the profile(s) to which this filter should be applied.

10. Click the Add button.

11. Click the Save Changes button.

For example, if you want to exclude traffic from a specific website, in Steps 5–7 you would select Exclude > Traffic from the Domains > That are Equal To. You would then enter the website domain into the Domain box.

Similarly, if you want to only track visitors to a specific subdirectory on your site, in Steps 5–7 you would select Include Only > Traffic to the Subdirectories > That are Equal To. You would then enter the desired location into the Subdirectory box.

Creating a Custom Filter

You're not limited to the three predefined filter types just discussed. Google Analytics lets you create your own custom filters that exclude or include data based on a number of different parameters.

The available custom filter parameters include the following:

- Request URI
- Hostname

- ▶ Page title
- ▶ Referral
- ▶ Campaign source
- ▶ Campaign medium
- ▶ Campaign name
- ▶ Campaign term
- ▶ Campaign content
- ▶ Campaign code
- ▶ E-commerce transaction ID
- ▶ E-commerce transaction country
- ▶ E-commerce transaction region
- ▶ E-commerce transaction city
- ▶ E-commerce store or order location
- ▶ E-commerce item name
- ▶ E-commerce item code
- ▶ E-commerce item variation
- ▶ Visitor browser program
- ▶ Visitor browser version
- ▶ Visitor operating system platform
- ▶ Visitor operating system version
- ▶ Visitor language settings
- ▶ Visitor screen resolution
- ▶ Visitor screen colors
- ▶ Visitor Java enabled
- ▶ Visitor Flash version
- ▶ Visitor IP address

- ▶ Visitor geographical domain

- ▶ Visitor ISP organization

- ▶ Visitor country

- ▶ Visitor region

- ▶ Visitor city

- ▶ Visitor connection speed

- ▶ Visitor type

> **NOTE: Custom Fields**
> You can also create your own user-defined parameters. Select either the Custom Field 1 or Custom Field 2 parameters and then define your filter via the Filter Pattern box.

To create a custom filter, follow these steps:

1. From the Google Analytics Overview page, click the Filter Manager link (beneath the list of website profiles).

2. When the Filter Manager page appears, click the Add Filter link.

3. When the Create New Filter page appears, enter a name for this filter into the Filter Name box.

4. Select the Custom Filter option; the page now changes to look like the page in Figure 17.2.

5. Select one of the following contingencies for your filter: Exclude, Include, Lowercase, Uppercase, Search and Replace, or Advanced.

6. Pull down the Filter Field list and select the parameter you want to filter by.

7. Enter the pattern you want to filter by into the Filter Pattern box.

8. If your filter pattern is case sensitive, select Yes for the Case Sensitive Option. Otherwise, select No.

FIGURE 17.2   Creating a new custom filter.

9. Go to the Apply Filter to Website Profiles section and select the profile(s) to which this filter should be applied.

10. Click the Add button.

11. Click the Save Changes button.

For example, if you want to exclude traffic coming from visitors with dial-up connections, you would select the Exclude option in Step 5, select Visitor Connection Speed from the Filter Field list in Step 6, and then enter **dialup** into the Filter Pattern box in Step 7.

Managing Your Filters

You use the Filter Manager page to edit or delete filters you've created. As you can see in Figure 17.3, all your filters are listed here. To manage your filters, follow these steps:

Filter Manager

Filters allow you to manipulate the data coming in to your account. You can filter out particular IP addresses, include traffic from a subdomain or subdirectory only, or create custom filters for more advanced requirements. Learn more.

Existing Filters			+ Add Filter
« Prev 1 - 2 / 2 Next »	Show 10 ▾ Search	◉ ◉	

	Filter Name	Filter Type	Settings	Delete
1.	MySpace filter	Exclude	Edit	Delete
2.	News.com Filter	Exclude	Edit	Delete

FIGURE 17.3 The Filter Manager page.

1. From the Google Analytics Overview page, click the Filter Manager link (beneath the list of website profiles). This displays the Filter Manager page.

2. To edit a filter, click the Edit link for that filter and proceed to the Edit Filter page.

3. To delete a filter, click the Delete link for that filter and click OK when prompted.

Summary

In this lesson, you learned how to filter your Google Analytics data. In the next lesson, you learn how to customize the Google Analytics tracking code.

LESSON 18

Customizing the Google Analytics Tracking Code

In this lesson, you learn how to customize Google Analytics tracking code.

Why You Might Want to Customize Google's Tracking Code

As you learned in Lesson 3, "Adding Google Analytics to Your Website," Google Analytics generates its data via a short snippet of JavaScript code that you add to every page on your site that you want to track. This code lets Google collect specific data about what visitors do when they visit your site; these data are then collated and displayed in various Google Analytics reports.

The basic Google Analytics tracking code works fine for most websites. But many sites can benefit from some slight adjustments to this basic code, to provide more specific or more detailed analysis of visitor behavior.

For example, Google's basic tracking code isn't optimized, out of the box, for ecommerce activities. If you want to track visitor behavior related to site purchases—especially if you use a third-party shopping cart—you need to customize the tracking code.

Equally important, if you want to track something that isn't tracked by default in Google Analytics, or if you want to track things in different ways, you'll need to customize the tracking code. For example, if you want to adjust the length of a visitor session, you'll need to modify the tracking code. You can also modify the tracking code to turn off the collection of certain browser information, for privacy purposes.

Editing the Tracking Code

Google generates a tracking code that is specific to your Google Analytics account. This code consists of two parts, each a piece of JavaScript.

The first part of the code initializes the tracking function by calling a specific Google Analytic's script (**ga.js**); it looks like this:

```
<script type="text/javascript">
var gaJsHost = (("https:" == document.location.protocol) ?
"https://ssl." : "http://www.");
document.write(unescape("%3Cscript src='" + gaJsHost + "google-
analytics.com/ga.js' type='text/javascript'%3E%3C/script%3E"));
</script>
```

The second part of the code activates the actual page tracking and sends that data to your Google Analytics account; it looks like this:

```
<script type="text/javascript">
try{
var pageTracker = _gat._getTracker("UA-xxxxxx-x");
pageTracker._trackPageview();
} catch(err) {}
</script>
```

(The "UA-xxxxxxx-x" is replaced by your actual Google Analytics ID.)

It's the second part of this code that you can customize. You typically do this by inserting additional **pageTracker** or event-tracking lines into the code, immediately after the existing **pageTracker** line.

Common Tracking Code Customizations

What tracking functions can you add by customizing the tracking code? Here are some of the more common customizations; additional customizations are described in other lessons throughout this book.

Identify Additional Search Engines

By default, Google Analytics tracks referrals from most major search engines, including Google (of course), Yahoo!, and Microsoft Bing. If you want to add other search engines to this tracking list, modify the Google Analytics tracking code by adding the following new line of code:

```
pageTracker._addOrganic("search_engine_name",
"query_variable");
```

Replace *search_engine_name* with the name of the search engine you want to track; replace *query_variable* with the query variable that search engine uses to initiate a query. (You can typically find the query variable in the search engine's help files.)

Use a Different Value for Inactive Session Timeouts

By default, Google Analytics deems that visitor sessions time out after 30 minutes of inactivity. This number may be too long or even too short for some sites. If you want to change the session timeout, add the following new line to the basic Google Analytics tracking code:

```
pageTracker._setSessionTimeout("xxx")
```

Replace *xxx* with the desired new timeout, in minutes.

Treat Certain Search Keywords as Direct Referrals

By default, Google Analytics treats all search engine keywords as organic keyword referrals—that is, it assumes that the links came from search results originating from user searches. That may not always be the case.

If you would rather Google Analytics treat certain search keywords (such as your own site name) as direct referrals instead of keywords, insert the following new line into the standard Google Analytics tracking code:

```
pageTracker._addIgnoredOrganic("keyword")
```

Obviously, replace *keyword* with the keyword you want to flag. Repeat this line to flag additional keywords.

> NOTE: **Methods**
>
> These are just a few of the many *methods* you can call from the *pageTracker* object. Additional methods are detailed in the Google Analytics Tracking API guide, located online at code.google.com/apis/analytics/docs/gaJS/gaJSApi.html.

Summary

In this lesson, you learned how to modify the Google Analytics tracking code. In the next lesson, you learn how to create user-defined visitor types for tracking purposes.

LESSON 19

Creating User-Defined Visitor Types

In this lesson, you learn how to segment your site traffic with user-defined visitor types.

Understanding User-Defined Visitors

In Lesson 6, "Tracking Visitors," you learned about the various types of visitor reports available in Google Analytics. One report not discussed in that lesson is the User Defined report. This report tracks visitors based on types that you define, by customizing the Google Analytics tracking code.

Essentially, the user-defined function enables you to label visitors by the specific actions they complete on your site. For example, you might create a visitor type for those who make a purchase from you or who visit a specific page on your site. You can then track the behavior of these types of visitors, as you would any predefined visitor type.

Creating a Customer Type for Visitors to a Specific Page

You define a new visitor type by adding a new line of code to the Google Analytics tracking code. When you add this new code to the tracking code on a specific page, it will label all users who visit this page as the new customer type.

For example, you might want to create different visitor types for users who enter your site on different landing pages, with a specific visitor type for each landing page. In this instance, you'd add the new code to the tracking code on each landing page, but define the visitor type with a unique label on each page.

This is the line you need to add to the page's tracking code:

```
pageTracker._setVar("label");
```

Replace "*label*" with the label you want to use for the new visitor type.

This line should be added directly after the existing **pageTracker** line. The resulting tracking should look like this (the new line is in bold for illustrative purposes):

```
<script type="text/javascript">
var gaJsHost = (("https:" == document.location.protocol) ?
"https://ssl." : "http://www.");
document.write(unescape("%3Cscript src='" + gaJsHost + "google-
analytics.com/ga.js' type='text/javascript'%3E%3C/script%3E"));
</script>

<script type="text/javascript">
try{
var pageTracker = _gat._getTracker("UA-xxxxxx-x");
pageTracker._trackPageview();
pageTracker._setVar("label");
} catch(err) {}
</script>
```

This new line of code creates a unique new visitor type for any user reaching the page where the new line of code has been inserted. It does so by creating a new cookie on the visitor's computer. The sole purpose of this cookie is to identify the visitor by the label you specified.

All visitors who reach the specified page will be tagged with this new label. You can then track these visitors with all of Google Analytics visitor-related metrics in the User Defined report.

Creating a Customer Type for Visitors Who Click a Specific Link

You can also create a new customer type for visitors who click a specific link on a given web page. In this instance, you add the **pageTracker** code to the source code for that particular link, via the **onClick** action.

The link code should look something like this:

```
<a href="link-URL"
onClick="pageTracker._setVar('label');">Click here</a>
```

Obviously, you replace *label* with the new visitor type you want to track, *link-URL* with the URL you're linking to, and *click here* with the text for the link.

For example, if you want to create a link to the CNN website (www.cnn.com) and track visitors who click this link under the "CNN Visitors" label, you'd use the following code:

```
<a href="http://www.cnn.com" onClick="pageTracker._setVar('CNN
Visitors');">Click here to visit CNN.com.</a>
```

Tracking User-Defined Visitor Types

All new visitor types you define appear in the Google Analytics User Defined report. You display this report by selecting Visitors > User Defined from the left pane of the Google Analytics Dashboard.

As you can see in Figure 19.1, all visitors of the types you defined are listed in this report. For each visitor, you see the following key metrics:

- ▶ Visits
- ▶ Pages/Visit
- ▶ Avg. Time on Site
- ▶ % New Visits
- ▶ Bounce Rate

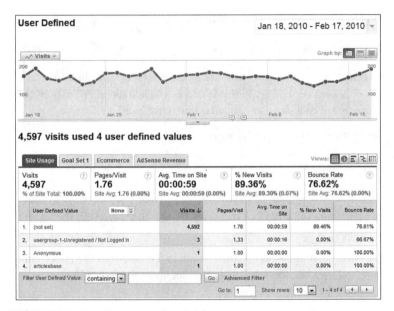

FIGURE 19.1 Tracking user-defined visitor types.

Click the link for any specific visitor type, and you display a more detailed report for that visitor type.

Summary

In this lesson, you learned how to customize the Google Analytics tracking code to create new visitor types. In the next lesson, you learn how to filter internal traffic from your Google Analytics reports.

LESSON 20

Filtering Out Internal Traffic

In this lesson, you learn how to filter internal traffic from your Google Analytics reports.

Why You Want to Exclude Yourself from Your Site Reports

Google Analytics does a great job of tracking traffic to your website—*all* traffic. That includes the visits you make to your own site or if you have a company site, the visits your company employees make to the site.

As you might suspect, this type of internal traffic can inflate visitor counts and pageviews and otherwise distort important data. For this reason, many webmasters prefer to exclude internal traffic from their Google Analytics reports.

There are two ways to filter this internal traffic, depending on whether you have a static or a dynamic IP address.

Filtering Traffic from Static IP Addresses

If you or your company uses static IP addresses, you can easily configure Google Analytics to filter data from these addresses. You can filter data from a specific address, or from a range of addresses, using the Google Analytics filter function.

Filtering a Single IP Address

Filtering a single IP address, such as your own address, is relatively easy.
Follow these steps:

1. From the Google Analytics Overview page, click the Filter
   Manager link (beneath the list of website profiles).

2. When the Filter Manager page appears, as shown in Figure 20.1,
   click the Add Filter link.

Filter Manager

Filters allow you to manipulate the data coming in to your account. You can filter out particular IP addresses, include traffic from a
subdomain or subdirectory only, or create custom filters for more advanced requirements. Learn more.

Existing Filters			+ Add Filter
« Prev 1 - 2 / 2 Next »	Show 10 ▾ Search		
Filter Name	**Filter Type**	**Settings**	**Delete**
1. MySpace filter	Exclude	Edit	Delete
2. News.com Filter	Exclude	Edit	Delete

FIGURE 20.1   The Filter Manager page.

3. When the Create New Filter page appears, as shown in Figure
   20.2, enter a name for this filter (like "Internal Traffic") into the
   Filter Name box.

4. Make sure that the Predefined Filter option is selected.

5. Pull down the first Filter Type list and select Exclude.

6. Pull down the second Filter Type list and select Traffic from the
   IP Addresses.

7. Pull down the third Filter Type list and select That Are Equal To.

8. Enter the IP address you want to filter into the IP Address boxes.

9. Go to the Apply Filter to Website Profiles section and select the
   profile(s) to which this filter should be applied.

10. Click the Add button.

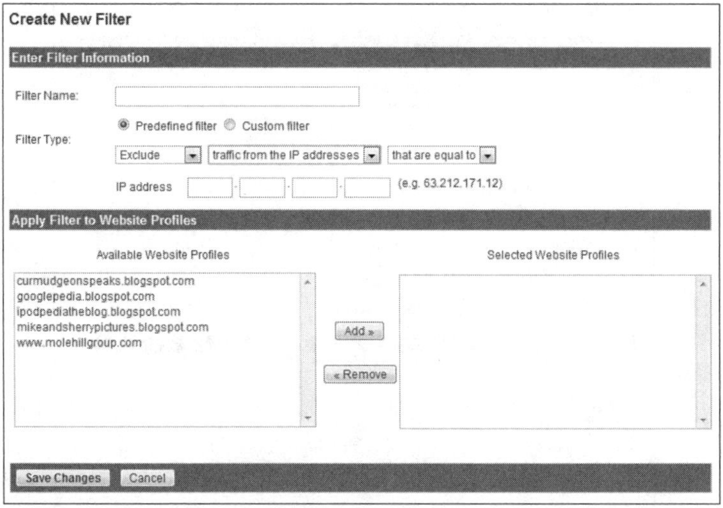

Create New Filter

Enter Filter Information

Filter Name: [   ]

Filter Type: ⦿ Predefined filter ○ Custom filter

[Exclude ▼] [traffic from the IP addresses ▼] [that are equal to ▼]

IP address [   ]·[   ]·[   ]·[   ]   (e.g. 63.212.171.12)

Apply Filter to Website Profiles

Available Website Profiles   Selected Website Profiles

curmudgeonspeaks.blogspot.com
googlepedia.blogspot.com
ipodpediatheblog.blogspot.com
mikeandsherrypictures.blogspot.com
www.molehillgroup.com

[Add »]

[« Remove]

[Save Changes] [Cancel]

FIGURE 20.2   Creating a new filter for a single IP address.

11. Click the Save Changes button.

Filtering a Range of IP Addresses

What if you need to filter a range of IP addresses—for example, for all employees of a company? This process is only slightly more complicated than filtering a single address.

Follow these steps:

1. From the Google Analytics Overview page, click the Filter Manager link (beneath the list of website profiles).

2. When the Filter Manager page appears, click the Add Filter link.

3. When the Create New Filter page appears, enter a name for this filter into the Filter Name box.

4. Select the Custom Filter option; the page now changes to look like the page in Figure 20.3.

Create New Filter

Enter Filter Information

Filter Name:

Filter Type: ○ Predefined filter ● Custom filter

○ Exclude
○ Include
○ Lowercase
○ Uppercase
○ Search and Replace
○ Advanced

Filter Field [Visitor IP Address ▾]

Filter Pattern [   ]

Case Sensitive ○ Yes ● No

▶ ⑦ Filter Help: Exclude > Visitor IP Address

Apply Filter to Website Profiles

Available Website Profiles   Selected Website Profiles

curmudgeonspeaks.blogspot.com
googlepedia.blogspot.com
ipodpediatheblog.blogspot.com
mikeandsherrypictures.blogspot.com   [Add »]
www.molehillgroup.com
                                             [« Remove]

[Save Changes] [Cancel]

FIGURE 20.3 Creating a new filter for a range of IP addresses.

5. Select the Exclude option.

6. Pull down the Filter Field list and select Visitor IP Address.

7. You now need to generate a *regular expression* (RegEx) that tells Google what the IP range is. Go to www.google.com/support/ googleanalytics/bin/answer.py?answer=55572, shown in Figure 20.4, and enter the first and last IP addresses in the range. Click the Generate RegEx button, and Google now generates a rather-complicated bit of code. Copy this code.

8. Return to the Create New Filter page and paste the RegEx code you just generated into the Filter Pattern box.

9. Make sure that No is selected as the Case Sensitive option.

10. Go to the Apply Filter to Website Profiles section and select the profile(s) to which this filter should be applied.

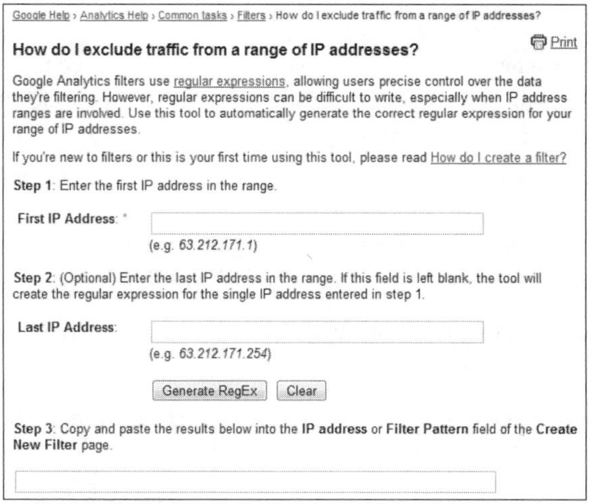

FIGURE 20.4 Creating the regular expression code for a range of IP addresses.

11. Click the Add button.

12. Click the Save Changes button.

Customizing the Tracking Code to Exclude Internal Traffic

Unfortunately, Google Analytics filters don't work if you want to exclude traffic from dynamic IP addresses. If you or your company uses dynamic IP addresses, you instead need to customize the Google Analytics tracking code—and do a bit of a workaround.

This procedure involves creating a new page on your website specifically for you or your company's employees. This page will contain a special cookie, which can then be used to filter visits from anyone who has that cookie installed. You or your company's employees must visit this special page to get the cookie installed, and then you can create a filter to exclude visits from users who have this cookie installed on their computers.

Here's what you need to do:

1. Create a new page on your domain. This page can contain any additional content you like, but it must contain the following code within the **<body>** tag:

```
<body onLoad="javascript:pageTracker._setVar('label');">
```

Replace the word *label* with the label you want to assign to internal visitors, such as "Internal Visitors" or "Employees."

2. Make sure that this new page also contains your normal Google Analytics tracking code.

3. Go to the Google Analytics Overview page; click the Filter Manager link.

4. When the Filter Manager page appears, click the Add Filter link.

5. When the Create New Filter page appears, enter a name for this filter into the Filter Name box.

6. Select the Custom Filter option.

7. Select the Exclude option.

8. Pull down the Filter Field list and select User Defined.

9. Enter the label name you assigned to the cookie into the Filter Pattern box.

10. Select No for the Case Sensitive value.

11. Go to the Apply Filter to Website Profiles section and select the profile(s) to which this filter should be applied.

12. Click the Add button.

13. Click the Save Changes button.

14. Make sure that anyone you want to exclude from your Google Analytics tracking reports (including you or your company's employees) visits your newly created page.

> NOTE: **Computers, Not People**
>
> It's important that you visit this new page from all computers you want excluded from your reports. The tracking is done by a device (a specific browser on a given computer), not by an actual person.

When you or anyone else visits the new page with the cookie, the cookie will be installed on your computer. Any subsequent visit you make to your website will be filtered from Google Analytics tracking results.

Summary

In this lesson, you learned how to filter internal traffic from your Google Analytics reports. In the next lesson, you learn how to track error pages and broken links.

LESSON 21

Tracking Error Pages and Broken Links

In this lesson, you learn how to modify the Google Analytics tracking code to track error pages and broken links on your site.

Why You Want to Track Error Pages on Your Site

Tracking the pages people visit on your site even means tracking those pages they shouldn't visit or had no intention of visiting. We're talking error pages—those pages that were linked to or entered directly that don't actually exist.

When a visitor clicks on a broken link to a missing page or enters a URL to a page that doesn't exist, they typically see a standard "Error 404" or "Page Not Found" page. That's not a good thing; you don't want visitors giving up when they end up seeing error pages instead of what they wanted to see.

To that end, you want to find and fix any broken links that lead to these error pages. Not only will removing broken links improve the user experience, it will also improve your site performance; error pages typically have high bounce rates, as visitors leave when they can't get to where they want to get to.

Modifying the Tracking Code

To track error pages via Google Analytics reporting, you need to add the Google Analytics tracking code to your error page template. Without the tracking code on these pages, Google Analytics can't report on these error pages or find the associated broken links.

For this to work, you must also make a slight modification to the tracking code. You need to edit the normal **pageTracker._trackPageview()** line to read as follows:

```
pageTracker._trackPageview("/404.html?page=" +
document.location.pathname + document.location.search +
"&from=" + document.referrer);
```

With this modification made, the full tracking code should now look like this:

```
<script type="text/javascript">
var gaJsHost = (("https:" == document.location.protocol) ?
"https://ssl." : "http://www.");
document.write(unescape("%3Cscript src='" + gaJsHost + "google-
analytics.com/ga.js' type='text/javascript'%3E%3C/script%3E"));
</script>

<script type="text/javascript">
try{
var pageTracker = _gat._getTracker("UA-xxxxxx-x");
pageTracker._trackPageview("/404.html?page=" +
document.location.pathname + document.location.search +
"&from=" + document.referrer);
} catch(err) {}
</script>
```

Once installed, this code sends a virtual pageview of the error page to your Google Analytics account. This includes the missing page name and the page URL from where the visitor reached the error page.

NOTE: **Virtual Pageviews**

A *virtual pageview* creates a pageview hit for any specific event, such as a Flash animation, PDF file download, and such. These virtual pageviews are then tracked the same as real pageviews in Google Analytics.

Creating an Error Pages Report— and Fixing Broken Links

You can track traffic to these error pages via Google Analytics Top Content report (Content > Top Content). Look for and click the listing for the **/404.html** page.

When the Content Detail page appears, you can see how many pageviews the error page received. To see what pages linked to the error page—that is, which pages likely have a broken link—click the Navigation Summary link. This page includes a Previous Pages section; these are the pages you need to fix.

Summary

In this lesson, you learned how to find broken links on your website by tracking error pages. In the next lesson, you learn how to track file downloads from your site.

LESSON 22

Tracking File Downloads

In this lesson, you learn how to track files downloaded from your site.

Why You Might Want to Track Files Downloaded from Your Site

By default, Google Analytics tracks *pages* on your site. But you can customize the source code of a given page to track *files* downloaded from your site; it's relatively easy to do.

Naturally, if you offer files for downloading, it's important to track those downloads. Maybe you have PDF files of instruction manuals, product brochures, or the like. Maybe you have digital music files for your fans to listen to. Or maybe you offer program (.exe) files for downloading, perhaps a trial version of a software program you also sell.

In any case, you want to know how many downloads took place and how visitors found those downloads. With the proper code added to those pages that offer files for downloading, you can track those downloads via Google Analytics.

Creating the Tracking Code

To track file downloads, you have to create a virtual pageview for the download. As discussed in Lesson 21, "Tracking Error Pages and Broken

Links," you create this virtual pageview by adding a piece of JavaScript to the link visitors click to download the file. This code must be added to every link that results in a download, whether that is a link within the page text, a link from a graphic button, or a link from a navigation menu.

Here is the code to add:

```
javascript: pageTracker._trackPageview('/downloads/filename'); "
```

You should replace *filename* with the name you want to track in Google Analytics reports; it doesn't have to be the actual filename (and should not include the file extension, in any case), but rather a name that makes it easy for you to track the file.

This code should be added to the JavaScript code that results in the file download. So, if the file is downloaded by clicking a link, you would add the **onClick** action to the link code.

For example, you would use the following code if you're downloading the file **example.pdf** from a normal text link:

```
<a href="http://www.example.com/files/example.pdf"
onClick="javascript:
pageTracker._trackPageview('/downloads/example'); ">
```

Viewing the Tracking Data

The code works by defining a virtual pageview for the filename you specify. You then track this page name in Google Analytics Top Content report (Content > Top Content). The page name you want to track is labeled **/downloads/filename**, as you assigned in the code.

The Top Content report lets you track a variety of metrics for the file download. You can track pageviews, unique pageviews, average time on page, bounce rate, % exit, and (if you have AdSense ads on the page) $ index. Click the link for the file download (or, more specifically, the download's virtual pageview) to display the Content Detail report, which displays additional metrics.

Summary

In this lesson, you learned how to track file downloads from your site. In the next lesson, you learn how to track full URLs from pages that link to your site.

LESSON 23

Tracking Full Referring URLs

In this lesson, you learn how to track the full URLs of pages that link to your website.

Why You Want to See Full Referring URLs

Google does a good job tracking other websites that link to your site—so-called *referring URLs*. Unfortunately, only the URL for the main domain is tracked, not the URLs of the individual pages that link to your site. That is, Google Analytics will report that **www.website.com** is sending traffic to your site, but not that the traffic is coming from **www.website.com/specificpage.htm**.

With Google Analytics default reporting, you simply don't know which pages on those referring sites are linking to your site. And this could be important; you want to know exactly how your site is being mentioned on the referring site. (Not all mentions—and not all links—are positive ones.) It's always good to see the exact page—or article or blog post—that is connecting to your site.

Creating a Filter to Display Full Referring URLs

If you want to track the exact source of links to your site, you need to add a filter to the basic Google Analytics data. Here's how to do it:

1. From the Google Analytics Overview page, click the Filter Manager link (beneath the list of website profiles).

2. When the Filter Manager page appears, click the Add Filter link.

3. When the Create New Filter page appears, enter a name for this filter (something like "Full URLs") into the Filter Name box.

4. Select the Custom Filter option.

5. In the list of contingencies, select Advanced; the page now changes to look like the one in Figure 23.1.

```
Filter Type:        ○ Predefined filter  ● Custom filter

                    ○ Exclude
                    ○ Include
                    ○ Lowercase
                    ○ Uppercase
                    ○ Search and Replace
                    ● Advanced

    Field A -> Extract A    [- ▼] [                    ]

    Field B -> Extract B    [- ▼] [                    ]

    Output To -> Constructor [- ▼] [                    ]

    Field A Required    ● Yes  ○ No

    Field B Required    ○ Yes  ● No

    Override Output Field   ● Yes  ○ No

    Case Sensitive      ○ Yes  ● No
```

FIGURE 23.1   Creating a custom filter to display full referring URLs.

6. Pull down the Field A list and select Referral.

7. Move to the Extract A box and enter .*.

8. Leave the Field B > Extract B list and box empty.

9. Pull down the Output To list and select User Defined.

10. Move to the Constructor box and enter **$A1**.

11. For the Field A Required option, select Yes.

12. For the Field B Required option, select No.

13. For the Override Output Field option, select Yes.

14. For the Case Sensitive option, select No.

15. Go to the Apply Filter to Website Profiles section and select the profile(s) to which this filter should be applied.

16. Click the Add button.

17. Click the Save Changes button.

Viewing Full Referring URLs

Once you've set up the filter, you can now view full referring URLs in Google Analytics All Traffic Sources report (Traffic Sources > All Traffic Sources). Normally, this report displays only domain names for referring sites. You can now, however, display full-page URLs in this report.

To do this, scroll down to the list of traffic sources on the Site Usage tab. Pull down the list in the Source/Medium column and select User Defined. You now see a list of full referring URLs.

Summary

In this lesson, you learned how to display full referring URLs. In the next lesson, you learn how to identify poorly performing pages on your website.

Identifying Poorly Performing Pages

In this lesson, you learn several ways to identify poorly performing pages on your site—and fix them.

How to Identify Poor Performers

Let's face it: You don't use Google Analytics to tell you how great you're doing. You use Google Analytics to help you fix problems.

Although a website can have many types of problems, from slow loading to broken links, the biggest problem is poorly performing pages. These are pages that are key to your visitors' experience or your revenue flow but, for some reason, don't do their job. These pages are poor performers because they don't advance visitors to the next step; instead, they encourage visitors to leave your site completely—which is not a good thing.

The key to identifying pages that turn off visitors is to look at the right metrics. For our purposes, the metrics that count are those that track exits from your site—the places where the most visitors leave.

With this in mind, you want to pay close attention to the top exit pages on your site—as well as those critical pages that have a high bounce rate.

Viewing Top Exit Pages

When looking for poorly performing pages on your site, you want to look at those pages that have the most visitors leaving them. These are your top exit pages, and they are tracked in the Top Exit Pages report (Content > Top Exit Pages).

As you can see in Figure 24.1, the Top Exit Pages report lists, in descending order, those pages that have the most exits. Your worst-performing pages, in terms of actual exits, are at the top of the list.

	Page	None ⌄	Exits ↓	Pageviews	% Exit
1.	/drum_pictures.htm		657	993	66.16%
2.	/tuning1.htm		650	710	91.55%
3.	/composing.htm		488	538	90.71%
4.	/hobbies1.htm		469	1,046	44.84%
5.	/		222	521	42.61%
6.	/hal_blaine.htm		177	198	89.39%
7.	/music_theory.htm		149	209	71.29%
8.	/ebay-templates.htm		108	116	93.10%
9.	/arranging.htm		96	115	85.22%
10.	/kenny_aronoff.htm		91	96	94.79%

Exit Pages — Views

Exits **4,597** % of Site Total: 100.00%

Pageviews **8,058** % of Site Total: 99.86%

% Exit **57.05%** Site Avg: 56.97% (0.14%)

Filter Page: containing ⌄ _____ Go   Advanced Filter

Go to: 1   Show rows: 10 ⌄   1 - 10 of 166 ◄ ►

FIGURE 24.1   Tracking poor performers with the Top Exit Pages report.

Raw exits, however, might not tell the entire story. Pages with many more pageviews, for example, by nature will have more exits than pages with fewer pageviews. For this reason, it's also useful to look at the percentage of exits—the number of exits divided by the total pageviews. To do this, display the Top Exit Pages report and click the % Exit column to sort by the exit percentage rate. Pages with higher exit percentages are your worst performers.

NOTE: **Percentage vs. Totals**

Which is worse—a page with lots of pageviews and a correspondingly high number of actual exits, or a page with fewer pageviews but a higher exit percentage rate? Technically, the latter page (the one with a higher exit percentage) is a worse performer, but the first page (the one with more total exits) has a higher impact. That's why you need to look at both metrics—but focus on those pages that have the most impact on your overall goals.

Viewing Poor-Performing Landing Pages

When it comes to deciding which are the most critical pages on your site, landing pages have to rank at the top of the list. These are the first pages visitors see when they come to your site. Quite often, these are pages you've specifically designed to display when visitors link to your site from an AdWords ad, YouTube video, or other promotional medium.

If your landing pages are poor performers, you'll never get visitors deeper into your site. You need your landing pages to retain visitors and lead them to the next step in the desired process.

As such, you want to look at those landing pages that have a high bounce rate. These are pages that visitors land on and then, before viewing another page, leave—for another site. There's something about a landing page with a high bounce rate that is turning off visitors; you need to identify what that is and fix it.

The first step in this process, of course, is identifying your top landing pages. You do this by displaying the Top Landing Pages report (Content > Top Landing Pages). As you can see in Figure 24.2, this report lists those pages that have the most actual entrances to your site.

	Page None	Entrances ↓	Bounces	Bounce Rate
	Entrances **4,597** % of Site Total: 100.00%	**Bounces** **3,522** % of Site Total: 100.00%	**Bounce Rate** **76.62%** Site Avg: 76.62% (0.00%)	
1.	/drum_pictures.htm	664	493	74.25%
2.	/tuning1.htm	649	603	92.91%
3.	/hobbies1.htm	506	280	55.34%
4.	/composing.htm	486	452	93.00%
5.	/	371	156	42.05%
6.	/hal_blaine.htm	179	163	91.06%
7.	/music_theory.htm	163	126	82.35%
8.	/ebay-templates.htm	112	105	93.75%
9.	/arranging.htm	100	88	88.00%
10.	/kenny_aronoff.htm	89	84	94.38%

FIGURE 24.2   Tracking poor performers with the Top Landing Pages report.

Next, you want to look at those landing pages that have the highest bounce rate. That means examining the Bounce Rate column (the far-right column) for those top landing pages that have the highest bounce rates. These are the pages that are welcoming the most visitors—and losing the most visitors, too.

Viewing Poor-Performing Checkout Pages

If you're selling merchandise on your website, a successful checkout process is vital. You don't want potential customers abandoning your site in the middle of checkout; these are lost sales, pure and simple.

To view those pages that have the highest abandonment rate, display the Funnel Visualization report (Goals > Funnel Visualization). As you can see in Figure 24.3, this report visually details any goal-oriented process you

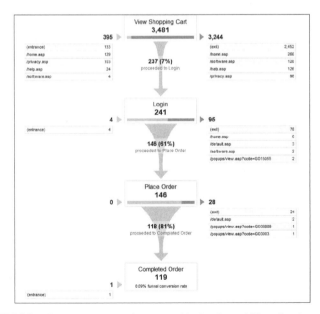

FIGURE 24.3   Tracking poor performers with the Funnel Visualization report.

configure. So, if you set up a goal of completing your checkout, and you identify all the associated pages, you can easily see which of these pages are leaking the most visitors—and costing you the most money.

Summary

In this lesson, you learned which reports help you identify poorly performing pages on your site. In the next lesson, you learn how to test page improvements with Google Website Optimizer.

LESSON 25

Fixing Problem Pages with Website Optimizer

In this final lesson, you learn how to test page variations with Google Website Optimizer.

Understanding Website Optimizer

In Lesson 24, "Identifying Poorly Performing Pages," you learned how to find those pages on your site that are losing visitors. After those poor pages are found, how do you fix them so that they perform better?

Google offers a great tool for testing possible changes to specific web pages. Google's Website Optimizer is a tool that goes beyond Google Analytics to help you not just identify poor performers but also fix them. It helps you improve your site, both in terms of visitor satisfaction and goal conversion.

How Website Optimizer Works

Google Website Optimizer (www.google.com/websiteoptimizer/) works by testing different versions of a web page. You have to first create one or more alternate versions of a page; then Website Optimizer will tell you which version performs the best.

What can you change? Virtually anything on the page is open game. You can change the page's core content, its design and layout, the organization of the content, you name it. In fact, you can create multiple variations, changing different elements on different versions, and then test each against the others.

Two Types of Testing

Website Optimizer offers two types of testing. Basic *A/B testing* compares two versions of a page, whereas *multivariate testing* compares multiple variables on three or more versions. Website Optimizer then shows visitors the different combinations you've created and reports which versions perform best.

Which type of testing should you use? A/B testing is a simple sort of test that is best suited to pages with lower traffic; it works best when testing entirely different versions of a page, rather than subtle changes of individual elements. Multivariate testing, on the other hand, works best with high-traffic pages (1,000 or more pageviews a week); it works best when you keep the overall layout and content the same and test changes to specific parts of a page.

Conducting an A/B Test

To use Website Optimizer, you first have to identify the existing page you're testing and then create and upload one or more alternate versions. All pages you're testing should lead to the same conversion page; you also need to identify that page.

> NOTE: **Multivariate Testing**
> Multivariate testing differs from A/B testing in that you test parts of the page, not the entire page. As such, you'll need to insert special tracking codes (generated by Google) around the specific content you want to track on the test page and then tell Website Optimizer what variations you're tracking. You can track multiple sections of the page independently.

With these important preliminaries out of the way, follow these steps to perform a standard A/B test:

1. Go to www.google.com/websiteoptimizer/ and sign in with your Google account.

2. When the main Website Optimizer page appears, as shown in Figure 25.1, make sure the Experiment tab is selected; then click the Create Another Experiment link.

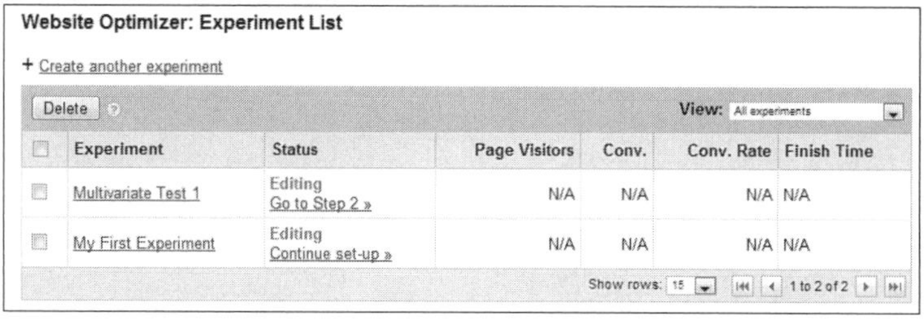

	Experiment	Status	Page Visitors	Conv.	Conv. Rate	Finish Time
☐	Multivariate Test 1	Editing Go to Step 2 »	N/A	N/A	N/A	N/A
☐	My First Experiment	Editing Continue set-up »	N/A	N/A	N/A	N/A

Website Optimizer: Experiment List

\+ Create another experiment

Delete

View: All experiments

Show rows: 15 1 to 2 of 2

FIGURE 25.1   The main Website Optimizer page.

3. When the next page appears, select the A/B Experiment option.

4. Confirm that you've created all the necessary test pages; then check the I've Completed These Steps box and click the Create button.

5. When the next page appears, as shown in Figure 25.2, enter a name for the experiment.

6. Enter the URL for the original page into the Original Page URL box.

7. Enter the URL for the test page into the Page Variation URL box.

8. Enter the URL for the conversion page into the Conversion Page URL box.

NOTE: **Multiple Pages**

You might think that A/B testing is limited to testing a single page. This isn't so. You can test multiple whole pages in an A/B test by clicking the Add Another Page Version link on the set-up page—although Google recommends having only a "handful" of variations.

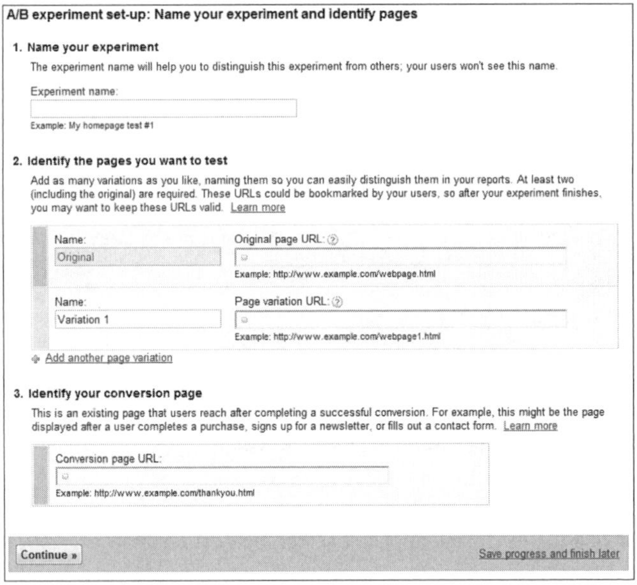

FIGURE 25.2   Configuring an A/B test.

9. Click the Continue button.

10. When the next page appears, select You Will Install and Validate the JavaScript Tags; then click the Continue button. (You can also opt to have your webmaster do this work; in this instance, Website Optimizer provides a link to the necessary JavaScript code.)

11. Website Optimizer now generates control and tracking scripts for your original page, the alternate test page, and your conversion page, as shown in Figure 25.3. Follow the onscreen instructions to copy and paste these scripts into the underlying source code for each page.

12. Once you've copied and pasted the tracking codes and uploaded the edited pages to your server, click the Validate Pages button.

13. If the pages are properly validated, select the Tags Have Been Added to Pages option and click Continue.

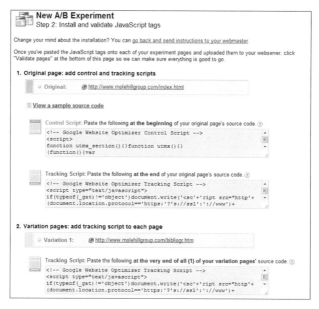

FIGURE 25.3   The tracking codes for an A/B test.

14. You're now prompted to select how much of your page traffic is included in the experiment; enter a percentage value.

15. When the Review Experiment Settings page appears, click the Start the Experiment button.

Your experiment now begins.

NOTE: **The Techie Guide to Google Website Organizer**

This lesson describes only the most basic use of Google Website Organizer. For more detailed instructions, download and read *The Techie Guide to Google Website Organizer*, available at www.google. com/websiteoptimizer/techieguide.pdf.

Viewing Test Data

Once your test is launched, data collection begins immediately. Of course, how much data you collect depends on your page traffic—the busier the page, the more data you'll collect faster.

You view test data by going to the main Website Optimizer page, selecting the Experiments tag, and then clicking the experiment you want to view. You now see the reports page.

If you ran an A/B test, you see a single report page, like the one in Figure 25.4. The top of this page tells you which test page has the best chance of outperforming the original. Beneath that is a list of key metrics for the test pages, including status (enabled or not), estimated conversion rate, chance to beat original, observed improvement, and conversions/visitors.

FIGURE 25.4   A typical Website Optimizer report.

NOTE: **Multivariate Reports**
As you might expect, reports for multivariate tests are even more detailed.

Use the information in this report to determine which variations (if any) are performing best, and then implement these changes permanently on your website.

Summary

In this lesson, you learned how to use Google Website Optimizer to test improvements on your website. This concludes our look at Google Analytics (and, in this lesson, Google Website Optimizer); hopefully you've learned how to use Google's web analytics tools to track your website's performance—and identify ways you can improve it.

Index

Symbols

% Change (Dashboard Sidebar), 26

% exit key metric, 5

% new visits (Dashboard), 29

_addItem( ) function, 116

_addTrans( ) function, 114-116

_trackEvent( ) method, 141

A

A/B testing, 198-201

abandoned funnels, 137

absolute unique visitors (Visitors Overview), 53

Accept User Agreement page, 16

accessing

    AdSense, 91

    Dashboard, 27

accounts

    Google, 9-11

    Google Analytics, 11-13

action parameter (events), 140

Actions (Dashboard Sidebar), 27

actions

    defining, 139

    methods, 140

    tracking, 139-141

ad campaigns, 105

    ad groups, 105

    budgets, 105

    charges, 106

    keywords, 106

    tracking, 107-109

ad networks. *See* AdSense

ad units, 92

Add a Gadget link, 18

Add "And" Statement link, 48

Add Another Page Version link, 199

H–I–J

K–L

Q–R

U–V

User Defined reports, 167-169

Using Blogger, 20

Using Google AdWords and AdSense, 93, 106

value parameter (events), 140

versions of pages, 197

viewing

AdSense revenue trends, 99

annotations, 49

checkout pages, 194

custom reports, 150

landing pages, 193-194

test data, 202

top AdSense content, 97

top AdSense referrers, 98

top exit pages, 192

URLs, 189

virtual pageviews, 180, 183

visit key metric, 7

Visitor Tracking, 51

Visitor Trending (Dashboard), 61

Visitor Type matches exactly New Visitor AND Time on Page is greater than 5, 46

visitors

browsers, 63-65

by region, 57-58

custom types, 167-169

direct traffic, 73-74

from search engines, 75-76

languages, 59

loyalty, 62-63

mobile, 66

network properties, 65

new versus repeat, 51, 58-59

referred traffic, 74

segmentation, 46-48, 54

sorting by landing page, 168

statistics, 54-56

tracking, 51, 167-170

trends, 60-62

unique visitors, 51

versus visits, 51

Visitors (Dashboard Sidebar), 34

Visitors dimensions, 147

Visitors Overview (Dashboard), 30, 52-54

visitors to a specific page customer type, 167-169

visits

versus visitors, 51

Visitors Overview, 52

Visits (Dashboard Sidebar), 26

Visits to Purchase report, 120

visualizing data, 152

W-Z

weaknesses of websites, 4

web analytics, 1-4, 7-8

Website Optimizer page, 198, 202

websites

ad units, 92

AdSense, 93

advertising, 91

SamsTeachYourself
from Sams Publishing

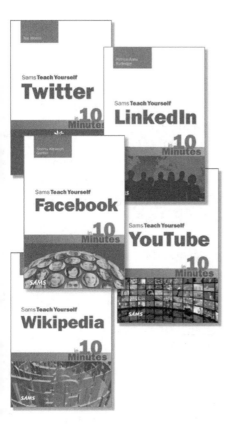

FREE Online Edition

Your purchase of *Sams Teach Yourself Google Analytics™ in 10 Minutes* includes access to a free online edition for 45 days through the Safari Books Online subscription service. Nearly every Sams book is available online through Safari Books Online, along with more than 5,000 other technical books and videos from publishers such as Addison-Wesley Professional, Cisco Press, Exam Cram, IBM Press, O'Reilly, Prentice Hall, and Que.

SAFARI BOOKS ONLINE allows you to search for a specific answer, cut and paste code, download chapters, and stay current with emerging technologies.

Activate your FREE Online Edition at www.informit.com/safarifree

STEP 1: Enter the coupon code: KBBXZAA.

STEP 2: New Safari users, complete the brief registration form. Safari subscribers, just log in.